THE VOYAGE OF THE MIR-EL-LAH

THE VOYAGE OF THE MIR-EL-LAH

LORENZO RICCIARDI

photographs by Mirella Ricciardi

COLLINS
St James's Place, London
1980

William Collins Sons and Co Ltd
London · Glasgow · Sydney · Auckland
Toronto · Johannesburg

First published 1980
© Text Lipat BV 1980 and
photographs Lipat BV 1980
ISBN 0 00 211887 4
Set in 'Monophoto' Ehrhardt by
Filmtype Services Limited, Scarborough
Designed by John Hawkins
Maps drawn by Tom Stalker-Miller
Copyright based by permission
of John Bartholomew and Son Ltd
Made and Printed in The Netherlands
by Smeets Offset, Weert

Frontispiece The *Mir-El-Lah*
in Cosmoledo lagoon, a lake
within the Indian Ocean

This book is for Mirella
if she doesn't know why, I do

And for Francis Madeka and Kimuyu Mutua
my crew from the hills of Machakos, Kenya

And for Roberto Vallarino Gancia
the Godfather of the *Mir-El-Lah*

And for so many who did so much for so little . . .
Domenico Ravera; Sheikh Mohammed Al Mak-
toum of Dubai; The Walis of Khasab and Masira;
Abdulfaz; Ari; Ahmed and Shaiyad of Khor-
ramshahr; Captain Barry Mitchell and the Bamburi
Portland Cement Company at Mombasa; Ali Sur-
uru, the Dhow Harbour Master at Mombasa;
Muriel Bonnet; Bob Zagury; Barry Allen; John
Galsworthy; Philippe Perrin; Jean Claude Favetto;
Sir George Hayim; Filippo Rusca; Luciano
Ancilotto; Tony Heckstall-Smith; Jeannot Bigot;
Hassan Soilihi; Lord Buxton of Anglia Television;
my thanks are also due to Maureen Freely for all
her help in the early stages and to: Adrian House;
Sonia Cole; Anne Harrel; Gill Gibbins; and for the
people of the dhows wherever they are.

Minolta Cameras have supplied the equipment to
Mirella, photographer: a Minolta SRT/101 with
35mm, 100mm and 300mm lenses

Foreword

The Ricciardis are victims of what Baudelaire called 'The Great Malady – Horror of one's home'. Neither can stay in one place. Lorenzo is a Neapolitan aristocrat who was born, he tells us, in the clinic of a Milanese jail. Mirella's grandfather founded the Panama Canal. Her mother was a pupil of Rodin; and she herself was catapulted into this world, in Kenya, on the shores of Lake Naivasha, where her father had crashed his plane. From time to time they have tried to settle down – in Africa, in London or Paris. Perhaps they will never succeed. For when Lorenzo writes of Arab dhows setting off like migrant birds 'at the first big blow' you may be sure he is also writing about himself.

Yet perhaps the Great Malady is not a malady at all. I – for what it's worth – believe that Man himself is a migrant species, along with the swallows and the whales, and that settlement is a perversion like any other. Man, alone among the animals, is a creature who trades with foreigners as an alternative to fighting them. And while some of our ancestors butchered each other on land, usually for want of understanding, others would put to sea in these beautiful ships with no protection but their skill and daring, and their trust in strangers. In such a ship sailed Hippalus the Greek, who came back with the tidings of Ceylon. From such a ship did Sinbad sight the Roc, and Gilgamesh the Islands of the Blessed. Ships such as these took Doubting Thomas to Malabar, Chinamen to Egypt, Hindus to the Horn of Africa, and Indonesians to Madagascar; and even with the present hysteria in the Gulf, the Voyage of the *Mir-El-Lah* was a unique experience.

The Belgian writer Jan Yoors once told me how he found an old Rumanian gipsy joining the puddles along a road with his stick. 'Water,' he said, 'should never lie still.'

Nor should – or do – the Ricciardis.

Bruce Chatwin

Contents

Maps and diagrams

Illustrations

Prologue

When I began my five-year voyage in the *Mir-El-Lah*, my Arab *dhow*, I hardly knew how to tie a proper knot nor whether starboard was the right or the left side of the boat. All I knew was that I loved the sea, and I hoped that determination, constant attention and common sense would get me through the first weeks. After that, I should have learned enough to reach my destination *inshallah* (God willing).

'Dhow' is a general term for those Arab wooden vessels which trade across the Indian Ocean. In fact this word is never used by the Arabs, who have many names to describe the various types of dhow. All are broad-beamed with shallow draught and carry either one or two lateen sails (in the days of Solomon and Sheba these were square and made of palm fronds). Dhows range in size from forty to four hundred tons. Mine was a *sambuk*, approximately fifty tons, with low curved stem and a high, built-up, square stern. With the double-ended *boom*, another type of dhow, the *sambuk* is the commonest of all these Arab vessels today. *Mir-El-Lah* is an arabised version of my wife's name, Mirella, but the Arabs generally knew my dhow as *Emir Allah* – 'God is king'. She was built in 1972 at Ras-al-Khaima on the Pirates' Coast, between the Musandam Peninsula, which belongs to Oman, and the Emirate of Dubai on the Arabian Gulf. I should explain that I have frequently used the name Persia as well as the country's new name Iran. Persia rather than Iran always calls to mind its thousands of years of history and the world of dhows.

I thought that nothing would be easier than writing about a sea voyage – it has a clear beginning and an end, a first adventure and a last. Between those two moments the sun rises and sets, morning follows night, and each day the boat moves closer to her destination. I have here telescoped a five-year Odyssey which may therefore seem episodic. When I began writing this book it seemed natural to begin with my departure:

'*I first set sail from Khorramshahr in the south of Iran bound for Mombasa on the Kenya coast. My final destination was Iquitos in Peru, up the Amazon.*'

But when I re-read these first lines I felt as though I were writing about somebody else, one of the many salty sailors like Slocum, Moitessier or Chichester who have described their travels – and I was certainly not one of them. What the hell was I doing as a *nakhoda* (skipper) of a dhow on the

Shatt-al-Arab (the river of the Arabs)?

At this point a friend came to my aid. 'Your story is not only about a sea voyage,' he said. 'It is about you and your way of life. First of all you must explain yourself.'

I was born in jail. The clinic of the prison of San Vittore in Milan was the nearest place my mother could be rushed to: she was on her way to Paris, where I had been conceived and where I should have been born. It was May 11th, 1930; I am a Taurian, the only son of an old Neapolitan family, perhaps a baron, probably a count, certainly a vagabond. My birth came nine years after my parents' marriage and I was oh! so very welcome. Years later my dear father jokingly told me that the only pleasure I had ever given him in life was nine months before I was born.

My mother died when I was seven years old – a doctor had diagnosed her peritonitis as liver trouble and four days later she was dead. I went to live with my maternal grandmother near Genoa on the Italian Riviera. She did not merely love me: she adored me. Too much adoration does not make a man out of a boy; but luckily she had an old-fashioned maid, Luigina, a tough, leathery peasant woman who could cook better, walk faster and scream louder than anybody I have ever known. She took me on long walks up in the hills of Liguria. When I ran out of breath we would stop and sit on the red earth under the shade of the big umbrella pines and I would stare down at the sea melting away into space.

I was raised a Catholic from my waist up. At the age of eight I was told I had a touch of the Devil: often during Mass I would blow my sailor's whistle to kill boredom; I sang merry tunes at funerals and cried at weddings. After shooting a soldier in the buttocks with an air rifle I was exorcised. First came a boring ritual, and then I was sprayed with holy water and left for hours kneeling with my hands under my knees on the cold stone floor of the Sanctuary of Divine Love near Genoa.

My grandmother had a friend, a painter named Guido Tallone, who always travelled with two large suitcases, each containing a woman's stocking. In his wallet he carried the picture of a beautiful young woman. He told me it was easier to live with photographs than with the people themselves; 'besides,' he added, 'I can change the picture whenever I wish.' He often came into the house through the window after climbing the wall outside. 'Never conform,' he told me, 'never! It kills the imagination. Until people say that I am raving mad I shall be fine. The fact that these same people buy my paintings for a lot of money proves that I am right.'

Another of my heroes was 'Uncle' Alessandro Cristiani, who was a carbon copy of D'Artagnan, the dashing musketeer. Tall and handsome, with a thick handlebar moustache and a goatee beard, he always swept into the house wearing a wide-brimmed hat and outlandish cloak. His passion was carriage horses. He also owned a yacht, and a Bugatti, gambled and travelled a lot, and kept many mistresses. Don Alessandro had a proverb about girls: *ogni lasciata è persa* ('each one left is lost'). Luigina told me he lived on the money of an old aristocratic lady and that I was never to use either him or his dear friend Guido Tallone as examples. Of course I decided to model my life on these two lovely, generous, smiling men. The virtuous ones I was supposed to admire were usually boring and sad-looking.

Quite early on I recognized that the maternal side of my family, the Gambarotta – my mother's maiden name means 'broken leg' – was very colourful, while on my father's side were the stability and common sense that I never wholly acquired. My father's father retired from the Army as a general in 1918 and died at the age of one hundred when I was thirty. My father, who was ADC to the Prince of Wales during the First World War, received a bomb fragment in his neck, a bullet somewhere in his leg, and a chestful of medals including the British Military Cross. Wars were common occurrences in my family.

In 1939 I was crossing the railway track that cuts off the Italian Riviera from its sea shore when I heard Mussolini's imperious and powerful voice from a nearby car radio announce the outbreak of the Second World War. '*La dichiarazione di guerra é già partita ...*' I raced home to tell my grandmother and Luigina. 'Oh my God,' they both said, and my grandmother added: 'We have had it.' Everything that was to happen during the next five years seemed to be reflected in her eyes.

My father took charge of a regiment of Sicilian peasants and after a few months he told me he had made them into the best singing unit in the Italian Army. He also helped them to write their letters home since most were illiterate. They were concerned with three things: the past, present and future virginity of their girl friends.

The fishermen of Genoa continued rowing out to sea during the first year of the war, and every night I would watch their bright *lampare* flickering in the distance. Once in winter, when it was very cold, I was allowed to go with them. I stared and stared into the deep water, where the area floodlit by the lamps filled rapidly with sardines circling madly in the light. Would I ever see a shark, or a giant squid ...? When I awoke I was at home in bed, where I spent two weeks ill with bronchitis.

During a bombing raid the house next door was hit. We moved to the country, where my great-aunt Carolina had a farm. We were surrounded by acres of wild forests, rivers and hills. My father gave me his shotgun, a cartridge belt, and some money to buy fishing nets. One of Luigina's nephews, Bastian, a tough eighteen-year-old peasant, became my constant companion. From sunrise to sunset we were out shooting and fishing, bringing home hares, partridges, quails, fish and river shrimps. We swam across the Po, slept under the trees, and caught fish with our bare hands. I shot my first wild duck and the recoil of the twelve-bore blackened my right shoulder for a week. They were happy days, when I could hardly sleep waiting for the next day to begin. Around us the war dragged on. The house in Genoa was badly damaged, and my father's apartment in Milan totally wrecked. Our villa in Rimini was razed to the ground; and, in August 1943, our beloved old house at Collina Pistoiese, as well as its private chapel and farmhouse, filled to the brim with family possessions amassed over the centuries, was blown sky high by a retreating German detachment.

My grandmother, Guido Tallone and Don Alessandro died. I had no more roots. I went to live with my father in his new flat in Milan towards the end of the war. I used to roller skate to school, the speed blurring the ugliness of the city where I was born.

I was shy and clumsy. One day while eating dinner in the beautiful house of one of my friends, Roberto Gancia, I spilled a glass of red wine on the white linen cloth. There was silence as everyone watched the stain spread across the table, and I made a decision. I would hitch-hike round the world, I would climb Everest, sail across the Pacific, swim in the Ganges and the Amazon. I would hear the surf pounding on the reefs of Tahiti and fall in love with a Vahine. Then perhaps I could spill a glass of wine without wanting to die.

Within a few weeks I was off; and after a two-year trip around the world I came back to decide about my future. My father bought me a flat above his advertising agency in Milan, but he might as well have bought me a gold coffin with a silver lining; I could have lived there all my life without leaving the building. I ran away, and wrote to my father begging him to try to understand. He did, and sadly sold off his successful business; I was his only child, and it seemed unlikely that I would fit into the 'Where-have-you-been-this-summer?' and 'Where-will-you-go-this-winter?' society.

I decided I wanted to travel with a purpose. A friend of my father's gave me a job with a film crew going to Hong Kong, and a few weeks later I set foot in China. On the return journey by steamer I fell in love for the first time. To me love came as a shock. I felt trapped. The lady in question, Veera, was a Pakistani from Karachi and she travelled with three hundred and sixty-five saris, one for each day of the year. She came back with me to Milan. I expected summer to last into winter; but the sunshine, the tropical moons, the pounding surf and swaying palm trees remained behind. I had stripped a dream naked; it died of cold.

I was then hired to film a documentary travelogue entitled *A Trip to Paradise*, and embarked in an ocean liner in New York bound for Haiti, Jamaica and Puerto Rico. I was rather dismayed when I saw the passengers coming aboard: six hundred American matrons between the ages of sixty and eighty, followed by trunks and trunks full of tropical clothing, bikinis, and see-through light-weight blouses. When we reached Port au Prince in Haiti I decided to remain ashore on the pretext that I wanted to film the departure scene. I set up my tripod at the end of the pier and watched with relish as the SS *Atlantic* disappeared over the horizon.

After a few years in Rome working as an assistant movie director, I found myself in Kenya to film the flamingoes of Lake Nakuru. One night in Nairobi, out of boredom, I went to a nightclub, the Equator Club. There were several charming whores, a few sleek pimps around, and some lovely photographs hanging above the bar. They were strikingly beautiful, Maasai and Samburu warriors mostly. 'Who is this extraordinary photographer?' I asked the barman. It was a woman, he said, and he had her phone number. I picked up the dented phone at the end of the bar and a voice answered, a warm feminine voice, deep, intelligent. Next day I met the voice and a few months later I married it. The years went by and we had two daughters, Marina and Amina. I have never regretted that phone call. Mirella's book *Vanishing Africa* (Collins, 1971) was later to contain all the pictures I had seen in the bar and which were the cause of our meeting.

A gamble on the stock exchange paid off and I made a large sum of money. I bought a sports fishing boat with diesel engines and a flying bridge, built to catch marlin, sailfish and giant tuna. I shipped the boat, called *Samaki* (meaning 'fish' in Swahili), to Kilifi north of Mombasa, where Mirella and I had bought a house on the Indian Ocean. I soon lost my money as easily as I had made it and chartered *Samaki* for a living. I became a professional fisherman, but after a while I grew restless and knew that something new, more exciting, had to happen soon.

PART ONE

Previous page This photograph by Wilfred Thesiger shows an ocean-going *boom*, sailing home to Kuwait from Zanzibar in May, 1949. It was this picture, first seen in a magazine, that caught my imagination and fired my determination to possess a dhow of my own.

1. The Dream

It was one of those motionless afternoons in April when everything is veiled in a shroud of heat, the time of the year when the east coast of Africa holds its breath, a period of silence between the monsoons. The white and purple bougainvillea bushes and the great baobab trees around my house stood out against the pale, hot sky, looking withered and exhausted as they waited for a breath of air to ripple through their leaves. Sibillo, my cat, lay panting on the straw mat beneath the rustic Arab bed on the veranda where I was reading. It was too hot to concentrate. The effort to hold up the book was too much and I let it fall to the floor. I looked out at the sea through the wide arches that frame the outer reef and the *mlango* – the passage into Kilifi Creek.

I heard a faint rustle in the bushes that flanked the tiny path leading to the beach. Three men moved slowly up the path; they did not see me. When I greeted them they looked at me in startled surprise; their haggard faces dripped with perspiration. They managed a tired smile when I asked them in Swahili what they wanted. 'We are in trouble, Bwana,' they said. One of them came forward and clutched my hand with both of his, bowing slightly as though he were going to kiss it.

The men wore faded *kikois* knotted round their waists and held in place with a leather belt. They carried *khanjars*, those magnificent curved silver daggers, fastened to their buckles. Limp cotton turbans were wound around their heads. Their weather-beaten faces, the distant look in their eyes, and their gnarled hands made me recognise them as sailors. They needed water: they came from a dhow, they said, and had been drifting at sea for ten days with a broken rudder. A passing *jahazi*, a small Lamu dhow, had brought them ashore and they needed help.

I told them to come in out of the sun. I poured them glasses of cold water which they gulped down. I refilled their glasses and then left them to find Said, one of my sailors, who was snoring in his hut. I told him to prepare *Samaki* in five minutes. Then I called Mirella, asleep next door, and told her about the arrival of the dhow people. I knew only too well what it meant to be adrift at sea with no water; I told Mirella to round up all our safari water-containers and fill them.

Within half an hour *Samaki*'s bow was cutting the water at twenty knots, sending a tulip of spray and sparkling white bubbles up in the air. The light was intense and hurt my eyes. In the distance I spotted the dhow, a black dot on the shimmering seas. As we approached we saw people crouching like eagles on the bulwarks; there must have been more than fifty of them. An excited chatter broke out as we drew near, and they greeted us with loud raucous voices. Mirella and I gazed at the bedraggled lot with the same curiosity as the men staring at us.

Bare to the waist, they wore dirty grey pieces of cloth and faded turbans; they were mostly tall and thin, with long sinewy muscles and sharp features, their glittering black eyes set in gaunt faces. I guessed the passengers were Somalis, and the crew were Arabs or Omani from the Arabian Gulf. The dhow was a *sambuk*, with one huge mast.

Their captain, the *nakhoda*, was one of the three men I had brought back with water and some timber to repair the rudder. It was only when we saw him among his people that we realized his rank. He gave orders in a soft yet firm voice; and the glances that he threw at his men and at the passengers as they moved the water-containers on to the dhow were enough to make everyone know he was in command.

As soon as the drinking-water reached the deck of the *sambuk* the men crowded round with tins in their hands; these were quickly filled, and emptied into their parched mouths.

A cargo of dried dates was piled high in the stern, with large cans of fat and dried fish. These were squashed under a faded green tarpaulin through which brown stains of sticky juice seeped on to the deck. Mysterious bundles wrapped in straw matting were strewn around, together with smaller packages of long rectangular shape – perhaps skins. Worn manilla ropes were heaped in brown hairy piles, and makeshift bedding had been arranged against them. Above all this mess towered the great mast. The tattered sail provided some shade. Sliced kingfish, their flesh orange and gold, hung from the spars and sent an evil stench downwind.

I tried to talk to the *nakhoda* using my sailor, Said, as interpreter. Said was a Bajun from Lamu Island and spoke some Arabic. Through him I learned that the dhow was out of Salalah in Oman, bound for Mombasa with a cargo of dried fish, dates and other merchandise. In a month or two it would load up with *boriti* poles in Lamu and sail home. I suspected that the passengers were mercenaries joining the Tanzanian Army – Somalis make good warriors.

When we bid them farewell they thanked us profusely, bending themselves in half and praising *Allah akbar*: He had heard their prayers, but I was the instrument He had chosen to save their lives. It was very moving.

That night Mirella and I sat for a long time under the stars talking about those men, their destinies – and their ship.

From that day on I became obsessed with dhows. I spent hours watching them in the old port at Mombasa; I waited for them to pass when the monsoon changed, filling their great lateen sails. I learned their names, recognising one from another – *booms*, *sambuks*, *jahazis* – studying their different rigs, the height of their masts, their measurements, and their crews. But about their world I learned little, other than that it seemed to be a vanishing one.

That summer I went to the reefs of Takaungu, near Kilifi, with a fisherman called Juma and some of his friends. He was a handsome fellow, never without his wide-brimmed straw hat. He owned a small sailing canoe – an *ingalao* – carved from a single tree trunk. It contained a sharp blade, a fishing line, one paddle, and half a coconut shell for a bailer.

On our frequent trips to the reefs we exchanged no more than a few words, yet from Juma I learned many secrets of the sea. He knew every current, fair and foul, the precise spot where the fish lay and the exact moment when they would bite. He fished in silence, never betraying his feelings when he hauled in the red snappers in twos and threes. At the end of the day he would paddle swiftly homeward with long smooth strokes, his line neatly coiled at his feet, the old hooks shining like new. (He had a few spare hooks, for often sharks would tear them from his line.) I compared his needs with mine, and marvelled at such thrift.

One day, when we had stopped fishing and Juma slept, I swam ashore across the reef. I watched the antics of a school of dolphins, delighting in the acrobatics of the youngsters leaping higher than their elders to somersault back into the water, sending up geysers of spray. I loved the reef of Takaungu because no one went there except for the seagulls. Now the tide had ebbed and, swimming to a cave at the end of the beach, I pressed my body into the warm sand, waiting for the flood tide to wash over me. It was then that suddenly I decided that one day soon I would own a dhow.

Later that summer my father died of a stroke. Only two days before, he had
sent me a postcard saying 'I am the happiest man in the world.' My daughter
Marina was with him when he collapsed in his garden. Her lovely face
framed by golden hair, her grey-blue eyes so like his own, and her slender
fourteen-year-old body were the last images he had of a good life.

A year before, I had finally persuaded him to retire; he had worked too
long, and I did not want to inherit all his money. Then, in his house at Nervi,
tending his roses, seeing old friends and watching the sunsets far from the
madding crowd, he had found a certain contentment. I had been able to
repay him a long-standing debt, concealing the truth that I was almost
penniless. Now I was the last of my family. He had left me his house, a vague
title, some money, and memories that flooded my mind as I wandered
through the rooms of his house – my house – after I had buried him next to
his own father and sister on the high hills overlooking the sea at Nervi.

I gathered a few things of value – an antique Florentine table, my father's
desk, old photographs and books, the painting that had hung above my bed
as a child – everything I could not bear to leave rotting in an empty house. I
packed them into my car, together with Mirella and Marina and Amina.
Heading for London, we were to see a publisher and talk about the
possibility of writing a new book or making a film.

'What do you want to do now?'

The man facing me across his desk asked the question I had put to myself
countless times since my arrival in London. He had already bought
Mirella's book *Vanishing Africa* and was interested in other projects we
might put forward.

'We will have to find a company to finance a film,' he said, 'and that would
also give you material for a book. Have you got any ideas?'

My thoughts flew thousands of miles away. I was standing on the
ramparts of Fort Jesus in Mombasa, watching the dhows sail into the
harbour with the last of the monsoon. I could hear the sailors chanting as
they dropped anchor and unloaded their cargoes of salt, carpets from Shiraz
and Isfahan, brass coffee-pots and water-jugs, and carved wooden chests
from the Hadhramaut. I was sitting on a Portuguese cannon; Mirella was
taking pictures of *nakhodas* anxiously guarding their cargoes, of small
ingalaos and of the fearless youths who climbed the masts and dived into the
sea. Some sailors sang songs strangely sad, nasal and dirge-like, haunting

and alien to my ears, the songs of men whose way of life was fast disappearing.

Of course I knew what I wanted to do. Coming out of my daydream I turned to the man at the desk and told him all I knew about dhows.

'They are the oldest sea-going vessels known to man,' I heard myself saying, 'and soon they will be as dead as dinosaurs. Fifty years ago the dhows came to Africa in hundreds; this year I could count only a dozen.'

It was agreed that we should make a film to help to underwrite the voyage and to record the last glimpses of the world of the dhows. In the end the practical difficulties of film-making and the many attempts to fuse our separate views on this world resulted in a film which was, to my mind, something less than authentic.

A few days later, with a film contract from Anglia Television and money in my hand, I agreed to go on a survey trip to Khorramshahr in Iran, to Basra in Iraq, and to the Emirates of the Arabian Gulf, exploring those ports still used by dhows. After months of inertia I had an objective and the hope of overcoming the depression that had persisted since my father's death. I did not have any illusions about the film business. Experience had taught me that while one may start with a vision, usually far too many people get involved for the vision to survive intact. I left to discover the world of the dhows. Would I still find it?

2. The Quest

When my plane landed at Tehran airport I shuffled through Customs
wearing a three-piece suit, hopelessly inappropriate for the edge of the
Empty Quarter of Arabia, perhaps my final destination. I began to realise
how swiftly events had overtaken me.

As I cleared Customs somebody slapped me on the back and I turned to
face my old friend Roberto Gancia, at whose table I had spilled wine when a
schoolboy. We had not met for years, not since he had gone to Iran to make
his fortune. Immediately he took me over and, as can only happen with old
friends, life began where it had left off.

Roberto's father had been one of my father's closest friends; he already
knew of my loss and did everything he could to lift my spirits. He flew me
sightseeing in his helicopter and arranged a horseback safari to hunt ibex
across the Elburz mountains that separate Tehran from the Caspian Sea. He
was such good company, I stayed with him longer than I had intended.
Together we planned my expedition to the south; with connections
everywhere, he assured me that all doors would be open to me and obtaining
the necessary permits would be no problem.

Khorramshahr on the Shatt-al-Arab was my first stop after leaving
Tehran. The 'River of the Arabs' – the Arvand for the Irani – is the
waterway of the Terrestrial Paradise, formed by the Tigris, the Euphrates
and the other lesser-known rivers like the Karun, which flow into the
Arabian Gulf. Across the river and to the north of Khorramshahr is Basra in
Iraq, and for centuries the two cities have been the centres of the date trade.
Peace and prosperity existed along the Shatt-al-Arab and the canals that
carried fertility to the interior. But the discovery of oil had destroyed that

peaceful existence: Khorramshahr was the base of the Imperial Irani Navy, and Iraq, militarily the weaker, had heavily fortified its side of the river. The dhows still ply their date trade along it – but only just: those flying the Irani flag keep to one bank, the Iraqis hug the other. But since the river is little more than a quarter of a mile wide, and there are many sandbanks, 'incidents' are frequent.

Such a situation, and the fortifications resulting from it, came as a shock to me when I was physically confronted with them. Without Domenico Ravera, to whom Roberto had given me an introduction, Khorramshahr would have been hell on earth.

Although Domenico was an Italian naval captain, married to a Spanish princess, he was now the French Honorary Consul at Khorramshahr; a dynamic character, he was respected by the officers of the Irani Navy and civilians alike. He was a man who could not live obscurely, born to be somebody somewhere, usually in a place of colour and wide horizons. His only fault – if it could be called one – was his insuperable optimism. He refused to recognise impossibilities. For him, red tape was merely a shoelace to be untied. And so, as he explained them to me, the complexities of the situation between the two countries seemed trivial. What did it matter that the Shatt-al-Arab was the Arvand of the Iranis, while the Persian Gulf was the Arabian Gulf to the Iraqis?

Thus, lulled into a feeling of security, having spotted a dhow anchored in midstream and flying no flag, I borrowed a red metal dinghy and rowed over to her in full view of the soldiers and sailors on either bank of the river. The current was strong, and I had to pull furiously on the oars; I didn't notice the Irani patrol boat until she cut across my bows, swamping my dinghy.

Six angry men dragged the dinghy aboard their boat, leaving me clinging helplessly to a rope. Finally, they hauled me from the stinking brown water.

Although none of them could speak a word of English, it became obvious as we sped up the river that I was under arrest, probably as a spy. Although I was furious at their indifference to my condition, I knew from experience that indignation never pays in such circumstances, so as they led me ashore and into a cell I held my tongue.

But before half an hour had passed a young officer, smiling pleasantly, released me and took me to an air-conditioned building where, at a door marked 'Commanding Officer', he respectfully saluted, wished me a fine day and left me.

An even greater surprise awaited me on the other side of the door where I virtually found myself back in Italy. The walls were adorned with pictures of Italian ships and posters of Rome; on the table lay copies of *Oggi* and *La Stampa*; even the uniforms of the officers confronting me looked reassuringly familiar.

'Do you speak Italian?' the senior official asked, seeing me eyeing the magazines on the table.

'It is my native language,' I answered.

'Well, that makes things easier,' he laughed. 'Now tell me, what were you doing rowing in that dinghy on the frontier between Iraq and Iran?'

They listened politely to my explanation, speaking occasionally in perfect Italian learned, I discovered, during their training at Leghorn. When I had finished my story they outlined for me the seriousness of the current political situation.

If I intended to move freely along the river I must obtain the necessary permits from the Savak – the dreaded Irani secret police – for the area was a military zone in which both forces followed the movements of anyone they thought suspicious. They warned me, too, that the occasional trigger-happy sniper might decide to test his skill on a tall blond European paddling around in a red dinghy with a camera slung over his neck.

'It would be better that you wear a drab fatigue uniform,' the Commanding Officer suggested.

And so it was that when I joined Domenico for drinks that evening I appeared dressed in a jungle-green uniform. He was astonished and highly amused. 'Now you really are a target,' he said.

The next morning I was given permission by the Savak to explore the date groves in and around Khorramshahr.

For centuries the Shatt-al-Arab has brought fertility to the coastal strips along its banks. As men learned that wherever they could lead water date palms would flourish, over the years they constructed a network of canals beside which they built their villages and planted their groves.

The further I explored the area the more I was struck by its primitiveness. I felt once again I had stepped back into the past. There were no roads, only rough tracks; the only means of transport was Venetian-type gondolas loaded with dates and vegetables bound for the *shatt* (river).

I walked through the silent groves, halting now and again to listen to the whispering of the wind in the palms; I noticed a pile of planks propped against a tree trunk. I had come upon a dhow under construction. Two rows of palm trees supported her embryonic hull, her wooden frame curved like the ribs of a great prehistoric skeleton. The water was too shallow to float

The *Mir-El-Lah's* 'godfather', Roberto Gancia (*left*), with me feeling more and more like a *nakhoda* (captain)

her: she would have to be launched into the river with baulks of timber at high water.

As I gazed at her with rising excitement, an old Arab in a worn grey *dish-dash* appeared from beneath the shade of a tree. Clearly delighted by my interest, he took me by the hand and led me to the large mud hut which was his workshop. The floor was carpeted with sawdust, and hanging from the walls and beams were the tools of his ancient craft.

On a table stood a beautiful three-foot model of his dhow. With loving hands he stroked its sides and with eloquent gestures showed me how its miniature sails were hoisted. Then he carried it down to the canal and placed it gently in the water. Rocking it to and fro, he demonstrated its stability. He filled its hold with little stones for ballast and called to an Arab boy who was watching us to load it with dates. He then pushed the model into the river, puffing and blowing to fill its sails.

'To Zanzibar!' I cried.

'Zanzibar!' he chuckled, clapping his hands. 'Zanzibar!'

Then suddenly his smile died as he sent the boy to retrieve the little model and carry it after us to the workshop, where he sat cross-legged on the floor, staring at a heart-shaped piece of wood that seemed to mesmerise him. His expression was infinitely sad: perhaps he was sorrowing for Zanzibar and all those distant ports he was now too old ever to see again. How frustrating it was not to be able to communicate with these people in their own language.

I had seen the birth of a dhow and I knew then that my film would begin here, no matter how long it took or how far afield I had to go to complete it. Now I would visit all the ports in southern Persia whose dhows I had seen in action in Mombasa.

Domenico had advised me to depend solely on air transport since the roads were poor – if they existed at all – and the sea routes were seldom serviced. My optimism proved stronger than his. I was not keen to use the facilities of the oil companies, I told him. Their jets and choppers and speedboats were invaders; any land they claimed had long since been deserted by the dhow people. I was searching for Sinbad, and I would follow him by using the same camels, dhows and routes he had.

The road to hell is paved with good intentions. Time was running short, but I allowed Domenico to convince me that I should fly with a friend of his, a French pilot, halfway down the Gulf to Lavan with a load of spaghetti. I felt sure that the island itself would have little to offer me, but from it I could reach the mainland and hitch a ride to the southern ports of Bandar Linge, Kung and Bandar Abbas.

We flew over the Shatt-al-Arab at sunset, the river and its countless little canals spread out like a spider's web imprinted in the sand. By the time we reached the estuary the desert had changed from red to muddy brown where the Tigris, the Euphrates and the Karun rivers discharged mountains of silt into the Gulf. As night fell we watched the waters turn green, then dark blue, then black. Everywhere below I could see the oil flares, their liquid flames never still, lashing the sky like dragons' tongues. Kuwait, to our right, was a country on fire. I began to wonder if I would ever find the dhows, or if I was not perhaps already too late. But the pilot reassured me they were still scattered over the sea like floating gulls.

The oil flares of Lavan illuminated the airstrip, an ideal location for a movie about extra-terrestrial beings, casting dramatic shadows over the faces of the small, dark men who ran across the tarmac to meet our plane.

'Here are your compatriots and here we deliver the spaghetti,' laughed the pilot.

On Lavan, a barren rocky island, a catering company from Venice had built a gigantic kitchen supplying Italian food to hundreds of rigs, wells, ships, barges and tugs all over the Gulf. That night we had a chance to sample the cooking: lobster, chicken, *tortellini*, *arrosto*, cakes, cheese, *zabaglione*, washed down with red and white *chianti*, champagne and *strega*. For the Italians, living on this bleak island for two years at a stretch without women, there is no other way to fight boredom except by eating, and eating well. They called the place the Club dei Cornuti – the cuckolds' club.

When they read my letter of introduction from Domenico they shouted 'So you are making a film here! Are you bringing Sophia Loren or Brigitte Bardot? We have plenty of food for all of you!'

Barely able to walk after my huge dinner, I staggered from the air-conditioned dining-room to an air-conditioned trailer and stretched out on the bed wishing that, like the camel, I could store all the food in my swollen belly for the two weeks of possible starvation that lay ahead.

Next morning I began to investigate my passage to the mainland village of Al Moka. I recalled one of the Italians saying he had seen a small dhow anchored a few miles away from their compound – Green Park, they called it – and he offered to drive me to see it. It was still there. The five Irani Arabs aboard came ashore to meet us, and after some brief bargaining with the *nakhoda*, an old man with a henna-streaked beard, we arranged my passage.

An hour later I was sailing in my first Irani dhow, a small *sambuk*. The *shamal* (north wind) was blowing hard, pushing us at seven or eight knots towards the south-east.

I watched the crew trim the lateen sail, getting the hang of things before gesturing my desire to take the tiller for a spell. But the men seemed indifferent to such a show of interest. I felt disappointed not only in their attitude but also in the smallness of their vessel and the fact that they did not look like the romantic Sinbads I had admired on that first drifting dhow near Kilifi – they wore old, shapeless European clothes. We shared no common language and my judgement was based only upon their clothes and manners. Like a boy who has read the fairy tales of the East, I still expected to find an exotic world of silver daggers and white turbans, failing to realise that what made these men so different was their knowledge of the ways of dhows and the sea, handed down from father to son over the centuries.

When at last they offered me the tiller and I began steering, the atmosphere changed. I experienced a wonderful exhilaration as the dhow came alive beneath my feet; my fingers tingled as I grasped the carved wooden tiller. I sensed an immediate *rapport* with the crew as they watched their strange passenger, realising that he was reasonably capable of doing what they had been doing since childhood.

Later, when one of them produced a fishing line, and I saw that its brass spool was very dirty, I took it from him and scraped it with my penknife. They gestured that it did not matter: if the fish were there, and Allah willed it, they would bite anyway.

'*Allah karim,*' I said ('Allah is merciful'), one of the few Arabic phrases I knew. One of the crew answered, '*Allah akbar*' ('Allah is great'), and, as the others nodded in approval, I knew that these words had won them over to my side.

How often was I to solve problems by saying *Allah karim* and *Allah akbar*! A friend of mine, captured in Kenya by a band of *shiftas* – raiders from Somaliland – owes his life and his genitals to his extensive knowledge of the Koran: when, after having caught and stripped him, the bandits heard him recite passages from the Holy Book, they let him go – naked and penniless, but alive.

It was not long before we sighted the village of Al Moka. A row of mud huts, a fort on the dunes, a sad-looking plain dotted with withered date palms and, in the background, a range of grey forbidding mountains. Heading into the wind, we anchored, and as the sail was furled I was struck by a searing blast of heat from the merciless sun.

I have rarely felt more ridiculously out of place than when I landed at Al Moka. Here I was, standing on a dune in the south of Persia, wearing long trousers, a long-sleeved shirt, jacket and sneakers, clutching two suitcases as useless as they were heavy. Two soldiers came to lead me into the fort.

We crossed the dunes. No signs of life other than the crows perched on the hump of a dead camel. My sneakers quickly filled with hot sand.

The white fort was small and picturesque, straight out of *Beau Geste*, with peep-holes, gun fixtures, colourful flags and sandbagged machine-gun posts. The temperature within its thick walls was much cooler, and once I had unceremoniously discarded my sneakers I felt more comfortable.

I presented my papers to a lieutenant, who threw my passport aside and became more friendly when he saw my permit from the Savak. As food, drink and cigarettes appeared, another gesticulating conversation began. By driving imaginary vehicles and making car noises I finally made it clear that my intention was to drive to Bandar Linge. I 'asked' about cars. He roared with laughter, pointing to a few camels outside.

Sensing my disbelief, the lieutenant produced a map. As I studied it I saw that the famous road I had expected to find skirting Al Moka ran many miles inland, on the other side of that forbidding mountain range I had seen from the sea. Gradually it dawned on me that the only reason Al Moka exists is because Lavan is a fishing and pearling area, and the pearling dhows use the harbour for anchorage.

But now the pearling season was over. The lieutenant took me to the beach and showed me the heaps of empty oyster shells. The season had been poor, apparently, and the pearls small; all the vessels had already left and the only way I could reach my destination was on the back of a camel. Counting on his fingers he indicated how many days the journey would take: a week, maybe longer.

In other circumstances the prospect of travelling in a caravan would have delighted me, but not now. The film commitments made it imperative that I should hurry.

I slept fitfully that night, angered by my stupidity, and wondering what to do. I woke at dawn to the sound of a bugle and was oddly cheered by its romantic call. I strolled around the village, which was no longer deserted as it had been the previous afternoon. The air was crisp and cool. A few Arab women, their faces hidden by black masks resembling hawks' beaks, their bodies concealed by ample *buibuis* of dark cloth, walked majestically through the dusty streets carrying water-pots and baskets on their heads.

I was still not convinced that there were no roads – but when I followed the only path wide and long enough to be called a road it ended abruptly after a quarter of a mile at a well. There, surrounded by thirsty camels, I sat down to reflect.

Suddenly I heard the distant noise of an engine. Leaping to my feet I ran down the road until I spotted a man riding a motor scooter across a field. Waving and shouting, I finally caught his attention. With frantic references to Allah and Bandar Linge, I begged him to drive me south until we reached the road. Shaking his head and clicking his tongue he said, '*Khalil*' – 'too small'. He pointed to the one saddle.

Despair made me positively eloquent. 'The machine is small but Allah is great!' I declared, partly in Arabic. Such faith and some cash worked like a charm and he agreed to take me as a passenger.

One hundred miles down a camel track is a long ride for two people on a scooter with one saddle, a flimsy luggage-rack, and two makeshift foot-rests. One hundred miles over sandy paths, stony river-beds and marshland would have been hard going even in a Land-Rover. Rather than sail back to Lavan and return by plane to Khorramshahr I decided to take a chance, in spite of the possibility that we might break down and be stranded in the middle of nowhere, with little water and even less food.

Two hours later Ahmed and I set out. He drove standing upright on the pedals and I sat behind him on the saddle clutching my two suitcases, heavier now by the weight of a can of petrol.

The sun beat down on us mercilessly, but we made steady progress. At first the track was hard and the land flat; the motor hummed reassuringly as we gathered speed. But just as I had stopped worrying the track disintegrated into a four-foot ditch and we went flying into the sand. It was an incident to be repeated many times during the journey, but we quickly learned how to fly at the right moment, landing as lightly as we could.

We spent the first night at an abandoned fort. When Ahmed had unwound his turban we settled under a shelter of dry sticks, sharing some tepid water and a few dry dates. The desert and the mountains changed colour rapidly in the setting sun – brown, yellow, pink, a flash of red, grey and finally black. I wondered if Marco Polo had slept in this same shelter on his journey to China, and speculated how long it would be before this lonely spot was invaded by cars and petrol stations.

It was still dark when Ahmed woke me. The air was crisp; soon the sky was lightening in the east, and the mountains to the west were tipped rose-pink by the rising sun. My romantic mood was shattered as soon as we mounted the scooter: the engine refused to start. Ahmed smiled; evidently this was a common occurrence. Dismantling the carburettor, he showed me triumphantly that it was choked with sand. In ten minutes he had cleaned it and we were off, moving over a seemingly endless desert.

The sun grew even hotter than the day before, but worse than the burning heat were the blisters on my hands and backside. I felt that at any moment my suitcases would drop from my hands and my hands from my arms. To keep up my spirits I hummed military marches like *Colonel Bogey* and repeated all Mussolini's slogans that I could remember from my boyhood: *chi si ferma é perduto* – 'he who stops is lost' – and *noi tireremo diritto* – 'we shall forge ahead'.

Ahmed did most of the driving – he was small and light and could crouch over standing on the pedals and leaning on the handlebars. All I had to do was watch for passing landmarks – a rock or a bush, a distant curve to be negotiated. When there were no landmarks I counted to one hundred over and over again, looking at Ahmed's backside. What a way to travel!

Night came again, and another torrid dawn was followed by another blistering day. I began to hate the scooter and what its black plastic saddle had done to me. Towards evening I spotted a large animal racing through the scrub. When it came closer we saw it was a jeep: we had at last reached the road. I could not sit down, nor could I stand up; I could only lie face down, supporting my chin on my elbow.

I paid Ahmed. '*Sucram*' I said, ('thank you'), and he was off. He had turned the scooter round to start his return journey immediately, and I watched his red tail-light zig-zagging between the bushes until it vanished. How long would I have to wait for a lift? One hour? One week?

Half asleep I recalled an incident that had occurred after my father's funeral when I was driving from Nervi bound for London. My car and its roof rack were loaded with all the things I had taken from his house. I had passed the Italian Customs post without difficulty, but at the French frontier they viewed my antiques with suspicion and finally insisted that I must turn back into Italy. My car had French export plates and therefore, they argued, could not re-enter that country. I was overwrought and in no state to argue. Furious, I revved up the engine and crashed through the light metal barrier into France. I was in the first tunnel when I heard the roar of the two motorcyclists chasing me; but the tunnel curved, and they failed to spot me before I veered off the road into a crowded building-site at the end of the tunnel.

I heard a humming noise. Once again, on the desert road in the middle of nowhere, my luck held. A truck pulled up and gave me a lift to Bandar Linge, the home of Persia's finest dhows.

Overleaf Approaching Lavan in the Arabian Gulf

3. The Goal

Bandar Linge – *bandar* means 'harbour' – looked like a ruined city, dead and forgotten for centuries; it reminded me of the German cities I had seen immediately after the war, flattened by Allied bombers. I asked the driver to explain such desolation. 'Earthquakes,' he answered.

'You mean recently?' I questioned.

'Two years ago. Many earthquakes here. Many, many people die here. Sometimes two years, ten, one hundred years. Always big earthquakes.'

These people were resigned to living with such natural disasters, patching up their ruined homes, accepting what the future might bring.

The driver dropped me outside an open-air café whose roof had collapsed. I sat down at a table in the sweltering heat amidst a swarm of flies. I was dead tired and coated in fine red dust. I felt filthy right through to my bones and I was still sore from the scooter ride – if possible, even more sore now that it was over. I was desperately hungry, but I felt sick and could not face food. My mouth was pasty, my lips cracked. I went in search of a hotel. There were no hotels in Linge.

I have circled the world more than once, slept on the bare earth, been shipwrecked in the Atlantic. During a solitary trek across the Rajasthan desert I survived for days with one bottle of Eno's fruit salts. Somehow I would stay alive in Linge.

By the time I had quenched some of my thirst there were about five hours of daylight left. The man who had broken the news that there were no hotels spoke a little English and owned a decrepit Russian jeep. I told him I knew there must be dhows in the area and I was determined to find them. I produced my 'Bible', *The Sons of Sinbad*, that wonderful classic by Alan

Villiers, and showed him pictures of the dhows. '*Baghlas*,' he said. 'OK.'

He drove me five or six miles to a marshy plain littered with rusty metal drums and rotting truck tyres and on to a junkyard of wrecked cars, where he turned right. The heat was so intense I could only inhale by sipping the air slowly, praying I would not faint. All that kept me going was my determination to find the dhows and then move on quickly – as quickly as I possibly could – and come back in winter.

We climbed a sandy hill, and from its summit I saw the Arabian Gulf three hundred yards ahead, while slightly to the left I sighted the harbour of Bandar Linge, home of the dhows I had seen in Mombasa. Half a mile out to sea lay a dozen big *booms*, two- and three-hundred-tonners, five of them with two masts. They looked dead, but I knew they were only asleep, awaiting the coming of the next season, the next monsoon.

The old port of Linge was a long scattered line of mud houses on the foreshore, each with its wind tower to catch every breeze before it spent itself in the land's heat. Open at one side, they face the direction of the prevailing wind; but at this time of the year there was no wind at all.

The beach in front of the houses was littered with dead, stinking fish. Great carrion crows, the size of eagles, hopped and quarrelled with outspread wings, feeding not only on the fish, but also on bloated donkeys, dogs and piles of human excrement. The stench was nauseating. To escape it, I waved the driver forward.

A mile further on we stopped and I walked along the narrow space between the houses, emerging on to the beach where I saw a big dhow under construction but obviously abandoned. There was not a soul in sight, and the guide explained that the heat kept everyone indoors sleeping. Indeed, the whole place looked as if stricken by a plague that had killed everyone off. Even the crows here were listless, as if sickened by so much rotten food. Many rested on the rooftops, wings spread, beaks gaping.

I looked at the sea, past the dhows to the horizon. My mind flashed back to Mombasa harbour where Mirella and I had first seen these magnificent vessels arriving, their sails filled by the *kazi-kazi*, their tall, lean, hawk-featured sailors in their flowing *dish-dashes*, the proud *nakhodas* upright in the bows eager to land and start their deals with agents and merchants. I looked at the desolation of the beach of Linge, and concluded that dhows and Sinbads should only be seen in action.

I heard the squeak of a door opening and, turning, saw a man in a white *dish-dash* coming towards me, smiling. As he drew nearer I recognised him.

'*Salaam aleikum*,' I called to him.

Overleaf left One of the many magnificent
nakhodas we met on our voyage
right Two visiting *nakhodas*: Akab of the *Moby Dick*
could have looked like the one squatting

'*Aleikum salaam,*' he answered, adding '*Jambo,*' the Swahili greeting.

He was the *serang* (boatswain) of *El Mansur* ('The Victorious'), one of the most beautiful dhows that ever sailed the seas. Mirella and I had been aboard her in Mombasa. He was followed through the door by a cow that ambled lazily past. We walked over to the unfinished dhow on the beach and sat in the shade beneath the poop. He asked me about Mombasa and my wife. We talked of the heat, the winds, the time of year. He told me he would probably be sailing in November. Our conversation convinced me I had come a long way on my journey, but not far enough. I was looking for a living trade, for navigators, captains and sailors in some busy port; for Sinbad alive, not asleep in a mud hut with a wind tower on its roof. I had been warned that many of the Sinbads I searched for had already gone to man the oil rigs, where the pay and the food were better and the work less hard. Our conversation in Swahili lasted long into the afternoon.

That night I slept in one of the most awful places I have ever struck. After that night things could only improve, I told myself; I had hit rock bottom. My guide had explained that travellers could sleep in the local hospital for a small charge. He led me there and left me in front of a crumbling building, its entrance supported by props like a coal mine.

Yes, there was a bed available. The man in attendance took me through a labyrinth of dirty passages with cockroaches racing in and out of the cracked walls feeding on the garbage scattered about the floors. He opened a door with a huge medieval key.

'Knock hard when you wish to get out,' he said, and locked me in.

There were five men in the room and six army cots. In one corner near the door the chipped enamel spittoon was half full. Four men were Iranis or Arabs; the fifth, the dirtiest of the lot, was a European. One of the Arabs was grossly fat and wore baggy pyjama pants. He was about to say his prayers, kneeling on a newspaper spread at the foot of his cot. The others just lay on their beds staring at the ceiling and picking their noses. The European was struggling to scratch his back with a fork and was the only one who paid any attention to me. He looked me over with glassy eyes.

I collapsed on to my cot clinging to my suitcases and fell asleep instantly.

I awoke at dawn feeling revived and ready to make for Bandar Abbas. The door opened and a man came in with a cup of tea for me. I gestured to the others. He shrugged his shoulders, deposited the cup next to my bed and left the room. When I had drunk it I had to bang on the door for a long time before I was let out.

At the entrance door stood a man who spoke French. He explained that this was a jail – the jail and the hospital were one and the same. Here the sick and the dying, the criminal, the murderer, the tourist and the businessman, all were welcome. Some paid, some didn't; some got out alive, others died. The state of the latrines made me shudder. What medical facilities had such a ghastly place to offer?

I hired a jeep to take me across another long stretch of desert like a lunar landscape to Bandar Abbas and once there, in a real hotel, I had a much needed bath.

I was depressed and I still had a very sore arse. I had failed to find a suitable location for my film, and Dubai in Arabia would be my last chance to find one. The next day I boarded a plane for Dubai and began to fear that my film might be a stillborn child.

One glance from the air at Smugglers' Creek, the grand canal that leads the waters of the Gulf two miles into the Arabian desert, was enough to make me certain that I had arrived at the right place at last. It was filled with hundreds of dhows; here I could make ten, twenty, a hundred films. I saw my future written in the stars above the creek at Dubai.

As soon as we landed I headed straight for the bazaar and bought myself a white cotton *dish-dash*, a headcloth, an old leather belt and sandals. I was too pale, too European, to look the part, but my beard gave me a certain distinction. It was imposing, and Arabs love beards. When I asked my instant tailor how I looked he kissed me on both cheeks and said, 'A man with a beard like yours is a man!'

Leaving the bazaar I strolled coolly down the creek as if it were my custom. I was Sinbad, one of hundreds of others, walking along the shore. No ordinary sailor. A *nakhoda*. For many years I had been looking for myself; now, in Dubai, my search was over.

But where was my dhow, where were my crew? Where were my slaves, my precious cargoes of frankincense, carpets, dates, gold *tolas*, guns, ammunition, salted game skins and sharks' fins? Was I to voyage to the Great Pearl Banks or to Muscat in fabulous Oman? Was I to reach Zanzibar and return with a fortune in *boriti* poles and smuggled opium, cannabis hidden inside elephant tusks? Or was there more money in trading Japanese scooters for fat camels, to feed the exploding population of the Emirates? Or taking television sets and mix-masters to Abu Dhabi, transistors to Kuwait? I could bring back five hundred goats from Baluchistan or trade them for oranges in Karachi.

The choice was wide, but still I did not have a vessel. There were hundreds of dhows around: *baghlas* from India, *sambuks* from Sur and from

Somalia and the Red Sea, *booms* from Kuwait and fishing *jalboots* from Ras-al-Khaima, loaded with fish traps as big as igloos. The creek was seething with activity, cargoes being loaded and unloaded. A constant stream of dhows arriving and leaving, their chanting crews hauling and heaving, their drums beating rhythmically.

I closed my eyes. The dazzling scene far outreached my expectations. Mirella should have been with me, sharing my excitement, taking pictures. Without them, who would believe I had witnessed such a spectacle?

I roamed from dhow to dhow and finally stopped before a beautiful *sambuk*. It was still unfinished, and a dozen or so workmen were chopping, drilling, hammering, carving. They worked with such precision and love that I felt I was watching sculptors rather than boatwrights. Between me and the splendid vessel lay some fifty feet of stinking, oozing mud, for she was still on the stocks. I was forced to wait for the rising tide in order to board her without ruining my whiter-than-white *dish-dash*.

I stood there mesmerised by her beauty. To my untrained eye, she seemed to be about seventy-five feet overall, with a beam of twenty feet. Her deck seemed big enough to play tennis on. Yet as an ocean-going dhow she was one of the smallest. For me, and for the film, she was the perfect size, for fifty tons of solid teak was all I could handle. My dhow – for I already thought of her as such – had a large square poop and graceful lines. On her six-foot stem the carved crescent-moon of Islam pointed proudly skyward.

The carpenters had spotted me and waved me aboard. As soon as the tide allowed, one of them slid down a rope into a dinghy to ferry me across. I climbed the rope ladder with ease and dignity: one cannot lose his dignity when wearing a *dish-dash*.

My visit coincided with their tea break, or perhaps was an excuse for one. As I sat cross-legged on the poop encircled by the carpenters I thought I must look like Snow White and her dwarfs. They were smiling, friendly men; prosperous in a prosperous place. Gradually, as we sipped the excellent tea, I began to notice their different features, recognise their different tongues, and was able to distinguish the Baluchistanis from the Pakistanis, the Dubaians from the Iranis and the Bedus. The contrast between these builders and the sailors, fierce-looking men holding hands and striding along the beach, was marked. The backbone of the fleet, they originally came from Kenya, Tanzania and Zanzibar. Ex-slaves, but not slaves as we know them, for I learned in the Gulf that to be a slave was a sort of honorary title. Precious, costly creatures, they were fed and housed and generally treated better than useless friends or idle relatives.

Kharg Island, the largest Iranian oil terminal.
In the Gulf we sailed from flare to flare

I was no longer in doubt that I had discovered the centre of the world of dhows. Yet I still had thousands of miles to travel before I could take a pencil and draw a map of that world, and in order to do so I had to buy this dhow on whose poop I was sitting drinking tea. That I had no money did not trouble me. Somehow I managed to convey my desire to buy to the carpenters, so that several pieces of paper covered with exquisite Arab characters were pressed into my hand. Yes, I gathered, there was but one owner, not fifty-seven, as I had feared. A long name was repeated in guttural tones, Abdul Rahim Godai, the man who held the key to my destiny.

Hajji Abdul Rahim Godai, second-generation Irani Arab of Dubai, a merchant and a ship-owner. When we met in the bazaar he was sitting on top of a pile of merchandise – in one hand he held a white telephone and in the other a calculator. Our meeting went so smoothly that for a brief moment I thought I had become fluent in Arabic. I tried to tell him of all the good things I had heard about him, to extol the beauties of his vessel and the hospitality of his country. But the miracle did not happen and all I could say for the millionth time was, '*Allah akbar – Allah karim.*'

I am convinced that this was why I was able to buy the dhow quite cheaply in only one meeting. All we did was to exchange promises. I promised to pay twenty thousand pounds in cash and he promised to accept them, giving me the dhow in exchange.

The negotiations were translated by Abdul Rahim Godai's son, who was studying in London and spoke English better than I did. But his father and I had an instant *rapport*, both of us accepting our young interpreter almost as a necessary evil.

I still believe that my clothes and bearing, and my faith in Allah, rather than greed and profit, secured the dhow for me. I was an inspired man, and the Arabs love people who look beyond horizons. That, perhaps, is why the dhows are still manned by sailors who listen to the wind and look to the colour of the sky. They do now have engines, but little trust is put in them.

My last remaining problem was a financial one. I had to raise twenty thousand pounds within a few days. The budget for the film would never cover that amount. However, in my present mood nothing daunted me; I boarded the plane for Tehran.

4. The Gamble

Roberto Gancia was at the airport to meet me. He had four pounds of caviare from the Shah's personal reserve in his office, he told me, and if I did not stay for two or three days to tell him all my adventures he would finish it off by himself. I had intended to stay in Tehran only a few hours before returning to London, but the prospect of spending a day with my old friend persuaded me to change my plans.

I sat in the anteroom of Roberto's office while he conducted his high-powered meetings; whenever he was free, he joined me in making paper aeroplanes and sailing them out of the window. Then, when the last of the visitors had gone, he brought out the vodka and the caviare.

I told him of my encounter with the Irani Navy in Khorramshahr, my scooter ride through the desert, and my horrific night in the hospital-jail at Bandar Linge. In return he told me of his almost incredible transactions involving billions of dollars, trillions of barrels of oil, and secret meetings with Russians, Americans and prominent Saudi politicians. All the time the telex kept on printing incomprehensible – to me – messages: 'Godfather sick. Brother very thirsty. Can you help? Three million barrels would suffice. Two rigs broken down. Adnan does it again. Mark VIP arrives Beirut 007.'

At last he asked the crucial question: had I found a dhow? Too excited to mention it before, I now told him I had found the most beautiful dhow in the world. It was mine if I could raise twenty thousand pounds.

Roberto produced his cheque-book and started to write a cheque. I tried to stop him, but he insisted. He wanted us to be partners. I could pay him back with the profits from the film.

'But none of my films has ever made a profit.'

'Never mind,' he said, 'the dhow is ours and we will sail her together.'

'*Inshallah*,' I added.

The nonchalant way Roberto handled money left me in awe. He had become so used to it that he thought nothing of adding a string of zeros to a number. I did not want to take his money, not just on principle but because it was too easy a way out. I knew a better way, I told him. All I needed was

Overleaf The Iraqi side of the Shatt-al-Arab at Khorramshahr. Behind the palms mortars and machine-guns were hidden

twelve thousand pounds to finance my system at the roulette tables.

I have never heard Roberto laugh so much. He just would not or could not stop. Half an hour and one bottle of vodka later he told me if I could make him laugh as I had just done he would hire me at twelve thousand pounds a month. Then, producing his pocket calculator, he asked me to explain how my system worked. I must have chips, a roulette wheel and a green cloth, I said.

We played a trial game and by four in the morning we had won a theoretical one thousand four hundred dollars. Roberto no longer laughed; he was convinced. To describe the workings of the system in detail would be tedious. However, in brief, it is as follows.

In Monte Carlo I had bought a book listing the frequency with which any given number or colour comes up during a year. My system, which concerns itself only with the simplest of bets – red and black, *pair et impair*, *passe et manque* – was based on statistics. Whereas the typical pattern one sees while playing roulette is, for example, two reds followed by one black, or three reds followed by two blacks, and so on, there do occur, of course, longer series of reds and blacks but with diminishing frequency. Whereas there are several hundred series of four or less red or black during a given month, there are only five series of thirteen, two of fourteen, one of fifteen on average. In other words, the chances of black coming up after eight reds are much higher than for black coming up after only three reds. The longer the series of red, the more likely it is that black will turn up next time.

Every gambler knows this simple rule. And since casinos are notorious for devising ways to keep their customers from 'breaking the bank', there is at each roulette table a limit to the stake one can place on an even-chance bet. Assuming there was no limit and you placed ten pounds on red, doubling your stake with each successive black that came up, you could go on for ever until you recouped your losses. Since there is a limit, one way of getting round it is for two or three people to play as a syndicate; in that way the limit can be secretly extended. This is precisely why such associations are illegal.

But it is not always possible for the detectives watching the tables to spot who plays with whom. Three well-rehearsed partners can work together so long as they play at different tables, never show signs of recognition, and act quickly when one of them sends secret distress signals.

It was agreed I should fly to London and join Roberto in Geneva a week later, while he found a third partner. He would provide twelve thousand pounds and we had one month in which to win twenty thousand.

In London I drove to Anglia Television 'Survival' headquarters in Park

Lane to deliver the news that *The World of Dhows*, far from being dead, was very much alive. Also, I explained, there was no possible way of making the film other than by acquiring a dhow, and in twenty-five days I would be able to announce that, *inshallah*, I had the perfect vessel. Anglia agreed to charter such a dhow for several thousand pounds.

When I told Mirella I was going to Geneva to win myself the dhow at the roulette table she simply said, 'You're crazy!'

Roberto telephoned from Geneva to tell me that his brother, Piero, who had just arrived from Rio de Janeiro on holiday, was to be the third partner. The idea of caning the casinos appealed to his sense of fun for, like Roberto, he did not need to win. But for me it was a matter of the very greatest importance.

We started off with five highly profitable and exciting days in the casino at Divonne. We played carefully, never deviating from the system. We won four thousand five hundred pounds, but we were worried that we would be spotted as a team, so on the sixth night we chartered a speedboat and crossed the lake from Bourcinelle to Evian. It was an exhilarating, chilly trip. I gazed at the snow-capped mountain peaks as we cut through the mirrored surface of the lake, certain that in Evian we were going to grab some money from the casino's big white palace. With it, we would pay for my Arab dhow now floating in Smugglers' Creek: a *sambuk* built on the lines of Vasco da Gama's caravel. The idea hit home as the sharp bow of our speedboat sent up a cloud of spray. I pronounced the name slowly in search of inspiration. *Mir . . . El . . . lah*. Of course, I thought, I have it! *Mir . . . El . . . lah*. It sounds Arabic. It has mystery and beauty.

'Hey,' I shouted to Roberto, who was covering his ears with his hands. 'Hey, I've found a name for the dhow.'

'You've found what?'

'A name for the dhow. Listen – *Mir . . . El . . . Lah!*'

'Mirella,' he repeated.

'No!' I yelled back. 'Listen, you idiot – *Mir* dash *El* dash *Lah!*'

'Sounds Arab!' he laughed.

'You've got it – it is Arab!'

'She'll love that!' he shouted.

'I owe it to her. She's put up with me for seventeen years!' I cried.

That trip to Evian gave me a name for my dhow, but nothing else: we lost. Our money remained in the big stucco casino, despite our peeing together against its glittering walls for good fortune. Our luck ran out. After hitting thirteen blacks in a row, we rallied round Roberto – but before we could stake our chips to help him we were approached by an employee who resembled Bogart in *Casablanca*. With a glacial, '*Je vous en prie*,' he dismissed us.

'You can't win all the time' was our theme-song all the way back across the lake. We had loaded a case of ice-cold Kronenburg into the speedboat and never made it to Bourcinelle. We got lost in the fog and arrived in Geneva at midnight.

I do not specially like beer but that night I got drunk on it. I was able to put our losses behind me, and slept happily, convinced that all would be retrieved.

The next morning Roberto drove me to Geneva airport. I took the first plane for London. We still had three thousand pounds in the dhow chest, despite Evian.

When I showed Mirella my winnings, she gasped and said, 'You won't land in jail, I hope?'

'No, it's all perfectly illegal,' I assured her. 'We are sharks fighting sharks. The casino doesn't allow three little sharks to get together to fight the big fat one!'

She stared at me, unconvinced. 'You dreamer! No system ever wins!'

'You're right – if you don't stop,' I said.

'Do you know when to stop?'

'Yes, when I've got what I need. Twenty thousand pounds.'

'Please, can I come to Divonne next weekend? I must see it for myself.'

Mirella flew with me the following Friday afternoon, feeling like Alice in Wonderland. We had lunch on the lake. *Truite au bleu* and *Liebfraumilch* and Irish coffee. The air from the Mont Blanc was crisp and cool, bright-coloured flags flew everywhere and all the cars were shining and unscratched. Masses of plastic people had 'money' written all over their rich clothes. They all looked so very respectable.

Mirella could not follow our activities in the casino. She sat at the bar, happy to see me from time to time.

'Are you winning?' she would ask occasionally, looking worried.

'Not so bad. We're doing bloody well, actually. Look at the bulge in my pocket,' I hissed, 'but for God's sake don't touch it!'

That day our luck held. We all did well and no one ever needed the assistance of the others. We dined like kings and the bill was astronomical. I picked it up and slipped towards the nearest roulette table. I scanned one of the players' note pads and realised the red had come up six times. I dropped one thousand francs on the black. It came out. I collected my winnings, returned to our table and paid the bill with the chip I had just won. A dhow crew would have lived for a year on that amount. Highly immoral, I thought.

Mirella left for London the next day. I gave her an envelope with a tidy sum of money. She begged me to stop playing, but I needed more.

Piero, Roberto and I drove to the Casino of Saint Vincent, near Aosta in Italy. Driving up the mountain pass I had a premonition. I told Roberto we should conclude our gambling operation as soon as possible. We needed only five thousand pounds more.

An hour later when we had made over three thousand pounds I told them we must stop and leave right away. I knew my friends wanted to stay. I could see it in their eyes. I had to give in. It was their money we were gambling.

The casino looked lugubrious, its customers cheap. That night we lost four thousand pounds, and made back half that much. Piero and Roberto no longer smiled. They were tired, yet a demon had entered into them. We played till our eyes were red and our hands clammy. When the casino closed we left for the airport.

Piero was flying back to Brazil. I handed him a cheque for the losses, but he tore it up. He said that it had been his fault. He suggested I make a lower offer for the dhow; he felt I would get it. '*Allah karim*,' I said, happy that our gambling days were over. We had made fourteen thousand pounds net profit in one month. The next day I picked up the telephone and dictated a cable to Domenico Ravera, Khorramshahr, Iran. 'Collect eighteen thousand pounds First National City Bank Dubai and buy dhow from Abdul Rahim Godai, love Lorenzo.'

5. The Dhow

I found the reply in my mail box. It read: 'Congratulations. Abdul Rahim Godai accepts eighteen thousand pounds. Dhow *Mir-El-Lah* now in Smugglers' Creek near new bridge c/o Seif Mohammed. Your baby now. Love Domenico.'

I made a paper boat out of the telegram; with a matchstick I made a mast, with another a jackstaff, and with a stamp a flag. With two cigarette papers I made a lateen sail and then said to myself, 'Right!'

The dream had come true. The problem now was to adapt it to reality. I looked at my paper boat and blew it around my desk from books to bottles and bottles to tray until it finally came to rest against the telephone. I put in a long-distance call to Mirella, who was in Nairobi.

'I'm a dhow-owner.'

'Oh my God! How do you feel?'

'Hard to say. I've never owned a dhow before. We must get busy. *Alea jacta est.*'

'What did you say?'

'I said the die is cast.'

'OK, don't worry. I'll soon be home.'

Then I called Roberto in Milan. He wasn't there, so I dictated Domenico's telegram to his secretary. I decided to set out alone – a decision I was to regret later, for I discovered after several weeks in a hot tent that I was not cut out to be a hermit.

At first, it was pure joy to be on my own. The sky over Dubai was blue, and after weeks of European greyness and smog the sun felt soothingly warm on my skin. At the airport I hired a taxi and told the driver to take me to Seif Mohammed near the new swing bridge. I was the only European in Dubai bent on spending rather than making money.

Since I had seen the dhow, they had been working on her according to Abdul Rahim Godai's wishes. The alterations I would have to make filled my mind as we drove on the swing bridge and down the new road. On the left a flat depression extended away into the desert. We left the road and took a track on a course parallel with the creek. Two miles and several deep gullies and bumps later we sighted some dhows beached as if the wind had blown them gently from the sea on to the sands. As we drew nearer, I recognised the dhow – my dhow – all freshly painted white below her waterline. Above it her oiled planks shone in the early-morning sun. Her mast, a bit thin, slanted forward. The tide was out; she was high and dry.

It was a good, quiet spot on the edge of the desert with only a few huts and shelters. A thin and tall man in a white *dish-dash* came towards me. He moved swiftly, and fortunately he was a man of few words for I couldn't understand what he was saying. He showed me over the *Mir-El-Lah*, pointing out the changes he had been making and obviously anxious to know what I thought. It was only by pretending to faint that I was able to show I was tired.

Together we went to the bazaar; I bought a tent and set it up on a solitary dune halfway between the dhow and the barracks where the Indian and Pakistani workmen lived. They invited me to share their water and food, showing me a large refrigerator in which they said I could store drinks, eggs and butter.

And so my time in the desert began. In the morning I woke to the sound of the carpenters. Raising the canvas flap of the tent, I would gaze at my beautiful dhow on the sand. Seif was always there, moving like a grasshopper, giving orders, checking jobs, answering questions. The basic languages were Arabic and Parsee – the Pakistanis and the Indians had to manage as best they could. Yet they had all been dhow carpenters for generations, so that little time was lost in explanations. They knew exactly what to do and they did it to perfection. Like sculptors performing an ancient art.

There were about fifty of them; Seif was their master. Early each morning he went to town in his lorry and returned with it packed with those men who were living there. Each carried his personal tools in a straw basket. They were mostly short, thick-set men, strong and hairy. Happy men in a happy country, they were mostly illegal immigrants from their homelands, Iran, India and Pakistan. Those living in the barracks were newly arrived single men, starting a new life. All were friendly. On approaching them I was greeted warmly and offered *chai* (tea), *chai* and more *chai*.

I would sit with Seif in the shade of the barracks' roof of palm leaves supported on wooden poles. All around us were stacked great piles of wood of different kinds. Good hard woods from Burma, Malaya and India. All the time he watched me and as soon as he saw me looking at the timbers he would launch into mime. Yes, that was good – *taijib* – strong unbreakable

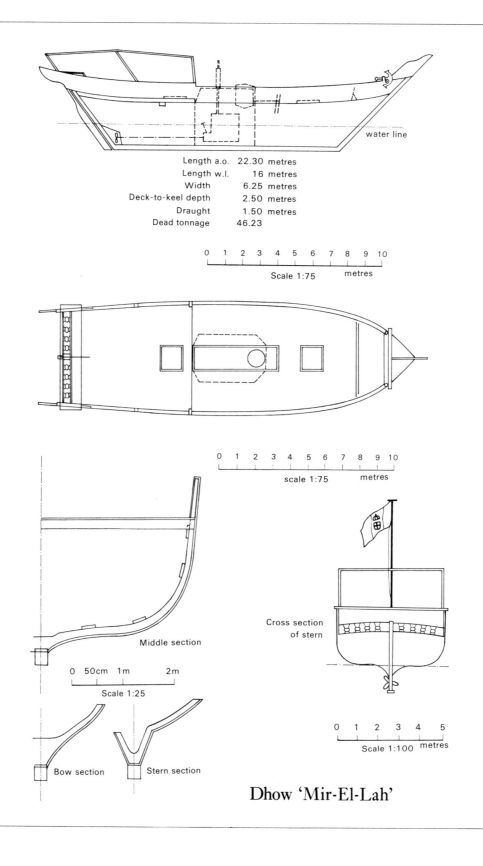

water line

Length a.o.	22.30	metres
Length w.l.	16	metres
Width	6.25	metres
Deck-to-keel depth	2.50	metres
Draught	1.50	metres
Dead tonnage	46.23	

0 1 2 3 4 5 6 7 8 9 10

Scale 1:75   metres

0 1 2 3 4 5 6 7 8 9 10

scale 1:75   metres

Middle section

0   50cm   1m   2m

Scale 1:25

Cross section
of stern

Bow section   Stern section

0 1 2 3 4 5

Scale 1:100   metres

Dhow 'Mir-El-Lah'

teak, number one, the best and no doubt about it. If my eyes rested on a whiter, brittle-looking heap, his expression would take on a look of utter disgust, the creases in his forty-year-old hawk-like face would deepen and his hand would move over his thin body as if to say such wood was frail and useless, fit only to build some weak frame of a worthless house.

'*Dhow lah, dhow lah*,' he would repeat vehemently.

Lah means 'no' in Arabic. Such wretched stuff was unfit for dhows.

Seif Mohammed did not remember where or when he was born. Of his youth he remembered the sea, the sands and the dhows. His father was a builder of dhows, his older brother was already helping his father. The brother of his father was building dhows. He came originally from Ras-al-Khaima, a few miles north of Dubai on the way to the Musandam Peninsula in Oman. Seif added, '*Taijib, taijib*.' ('Good, good.')

I longed to be able to talk freely with him and his men. The language barrier was a great problem, and I wanted to know so much. There was a wealth of tales to hear from them. Since they themselves scarcely understood each other, what hope was there for me?

The oil era had arrived and the old traditions were dying fast. I did not then fully realise that I was just in time to catch the end of the dhows.

My first priority was to find a willing and intelligent interpreter. Abdullah, Abdul Rahim Godai's son, was perfect. Seif brought him back from town. I drew a dhow in the sand and tried to explain my needs to him.

My main task was to convert a fishing dhow into a passenger dhow. Her bulwarks had to be raised considerably so that I could use her for my long-range voyages. The alteration would result in a drier vessel, the better to withstand the full force of the *shamal* and the south-easterly gales of the Indian Ocean. I had to alter bulkheads and open six ports (windows) in the high square stern. I had to build cabins, bunks, partitions, and crew quarters. Air had to be brought below deck if we were to survive a hundred and twenty-three degrees in the shade. I had to fit a shower and long-range water-tanks. On and on it went.

Since I wished to sail as much as possible, I had to increase her sail area, add a bowsprit, provide a jib, install a winch or two to save manpower. Winches had to be powerful enough to hoist the sixty-foot lateen *boom* and raise the heavy anchors. Every alteration called for careful planning. I had to keep the engine fumes out of the way, eliminate the exhaust-pipe with its horrible-looking smoke-stack built on deck, and to preserve the graceful lines from the contamination of the engine. The exhaust-pipe had to be remade by running a rubber tube below all the way to the stern. I needed a knowledge I did not possess, but Seif had all the answers, Allah be praised.

After drawing in the sand, the four carpenters and myself climbed aboard. These four carpenters were to work for me for a month. I shook hands with them and asked each one his name.

We had lunch inside the barracks where a young Indian boy was stirring a large tin pan brimming with rice and curry. Kabul spoke to him and he heaped a plate for me. Then he cleaned a spoon with water and gave it to me, holding it by its stem. I tried to pay. Kabul refused, but I insisted, explaining that I would be there for many days, even weeks. I suspected the food was paid for by a co-operative set up by the workers. The boy finally accepted the money and I knew where my future lunches would be made ready for me.

Replete, I fell asleep until at last the hammering woke me. Khan and Kabul needed me from time to time. I knew so little and they so much; but they were making alterations unfamiliar to them and thus we lost precious time. We could not communicate and there were moments when explanations were all-important. Beams were there for a specific purpose which I did not understand. At one point, I wanted a small piece of wood fixed to the deck of the fore cabin removed. Kabul shouted no, no, no, and laughed as he pointed to the great mast above. Only then did I realise that the entire weight of the mast needed that seemingly useless scrap of wood, the size of a cigarette packet, to stay in position.

There are many such situations aboard dhows, for their construction is at once simple and practical, unchanged throughout the centuries. A small hand-forged ring nailed to the deck is essential to hoist and hold the *boom* carrying a sail weighing hundreds of pounds. A dhow's fittings and riggings are made to withstand the test of time and are heavy. There are no instruments to measure stresses, strains or breaking-points. If such essentials are not right, you drown. The 'instruments' to test a dhow are storms, waves, winds and reefs, and they do not give a second chance. So the Arabs, the Pakistanis, the Indians, the Omanis, build their vessels for strength to fight strength.

By watching these people at work one learns that strength does not mean brute force. These carpenters have the wings of genius and they cannot afford to fail. The rudder of the *Mir-El-Lah* was astonishingly small. I felt it could not turn a five-foot outboard. Yet when I came to sail her I had to rig a block and tackle to handle it in a strong *shamal*. Only then did I understand what Seif meant when he told me about the size of the rudder.

'*Khalil?*' he said. '*Lah, lah, kebir.*' ('Small? No, no, big.') Then he interlocked his gnarled fingers and, moving them, shook his thin, long, dry hands, saying '*kebir*', meaning 'big and strong'.

Seif suggested I should fit a wheel in place of the tiller. He went with me into the town, and for the first time I saw the real Dubai. Now I was a man of the dhows. We selected a good wheel with carved spokes of hard Indian wood, brass fittings and rings, all made by hand, carved by hand, forged by hand. I should really say 'by finger', a refinement over things made merely by hand. Dhows and their fittings are all made with fingers. All you need to do to realise this is to look at the fingers of the workmen and the way they touch, feel and caress the wood or the forged brass and steel. A dhow is carved from wood, rather than just built of it.

That afternoon I watched Seif inside the white Arab house 'feel' a beautiful four-foot wheel. He caressed its oiled wood, checking it for cracks, looking for an excuse to strike a bargain.

'Sixty pounds,' the tall man in the *dish-dash* asked.

'Forty,' came the ritual answer from Seif.

Silence. The white walls of the large room, a wooden desk, a carved dhow wheel leaning against the wall and two white-robed Arabs about to make a deal. All I could do was watch. Seif stroked the wheel. He had found grounds for bargaining: one spoke had a small chip in it. Triumphantly, he took the merchant's hand and pressed his fingers to the tiny mark.

'Fifty,' the merchant said with great dignity. Seif paid him. The wheel was ours.

I asked Seif to drop me on the creek across from the Sheik Rashid Palace. He drove off with the wheel on the seat beside him, insisting that the metal floor of the lorry was not a fit place for an object of such beauty.

It is hard to describe a place where so much happens. You may start off by talking of the dozens and dozens of dhows lying five abreast alongside the cement pier that runs for two miles into the desert, where it dissolves with the water of the creek into the clean light-brown sand. There are all types of dhows flying the flags of their emirates, sultanates and sheikhdoms. There are, also, many new steel vessels, utility vessels, with spacious decks and huge, powerful engines. One rig looked for all the world like the Eiffel Tower lying on its side on giant barges, being pulled by a tugboat towards the open sea.

I sat with Kabul and Khan. It was the Arab Friday, their day off. Other pyjama-clad men came round to sit with us on the soft sand. We exchanged glances. We understood and loved each other. I bought a soda for everyone.

Overleaf Ahmed (*right*) was to me what Virgil was to Dante.
Shaiyad (*left*), my *sekoni* (helmsman) from Khorramshahr,
accompanied us to the Pirates' Coast

Around us, the wooden barracks, the remains of dead dhows – skeletons with spitted guts; old rusty engine blocks, water- and diesel-tanks, drums and old truck tyres. Beyond us, the desert. And, twenty miles inland, the sand dunes – and further away still the Ruus Al Jabal, the 'heads' of the mountains, the coastline I should soon follow.

The cook for the dhow people's desert co-operative spoke some English. He joined us. His name was Kharim. He interpreted for me. Another sailor came and he sat next to Kabul and Khan. He had come to look at his dhow in need of *calafat* (' to calafat' means to fill the cracks between the planking with oiled cotton strips, to make the hull and deck watertight).

'*Sucram*,' he said, putting his right hand on his heart, and setting his bottle into the sand so that it would not spill.

I was curious to know more about these men: their homes, their marriages, their lives. I asked Kharim to translate for me as I spoke to another sailor called Mohammed.

'How old are you, Mohammed?'

'Twenty-seven.'

'Where were you born?'

'Abu Dhabi.'

'Is your mother alive, and your father?'

'Yes, my mother. But not my father. He died at sea some years ago – where, I do not know. *Allah karim*.'

Here Kabul interrupted. 'Many hundreds of people die at sea every year. Maybe three hundred, maybe four.'

So Kabul told it to Kharim, who repeated it to me as best he could in fractured English, patching it with drawings in the sand.

Mohammed's father had been a *sekoni* (helmsman) on a very old and leaky dhow carrying illegal immigrants from a place south of Goa. Just as with the slave traders of old, such dhows were packed with men like sardines in a tin. They set out for Arabia, Oman and the Emirates, the promised lands, because in their homelands they faced death by starvation. From time to time a rotten plank splits, gives way, and the water pours in. If the seas are heavy, panic sets in and the dhow founders on its way to the Strait of Hormuz. The sharks clean up the mess. *Allah akbar, Allah karim*.

When a dhow sinks off the coast, many bodies are washed up on the shore and for several weeks the beaches are littered with debris. Kabul told me they had found three bodies on the way to Ras-al-Khaima the night before. More would be found today, more tomorrow. *Allah karim*.

Thus Mohammed's father had died.

All the men around me had run the gauntlet. Some, like Kabul, had done well. He had brought over his family; he owned a room on the outskirts of Dubai, and was putting away a tidy sum in the coffers of the British Bank of the Middle East. He showed me his savings book, nodding with satisfaction. Khan was all right too. The job on my dhow was his last. Soon he would be off in a good, fast Pakistani dhow to fetch his family; for the first time, I saw Khan smile.

I asked what kind of papers they possessed, what identity. Kabul showed me his. He had been in Dubai two years now and his skill had given him status. Papers were blank until some willing person wrote on them, and money helped to find such a person.

But what of the newly arrived? 'And how about him?' I questioned, pointing to a little man listening, his chin resting on his knees.

His story was almost the same as Mohammed's, except that he did not know where he had been born or when. He had left no family behind. He had no skills, but could sail a dhow, for he had been fishing and working in dhows as long as he could remember.

'Is he a good sailor?' I asked.

'Yes.'

In that case he could come with me when the *Mir-El-Lah* was ready for sea. Had he a name?

Yes, 'Saker'. But who had given it him he did not know.

So Saker had no form of identity. He knew he was Indian because that was his language. He looked about twenty-five and his life was what he remembered of it.

Kharim added it was the same for him as for many thousands of the coastal people. The sea helps a lot, he said. It feeds people, it is too vast for people to control other people. It is a good place to hide in. But there are many rotten dhows, he explained, and if you sink you almost always drown.

I asked him how it was possible for so many people to be in the country illegally. He answered that the Arabs were good. They needed people to do many tasks. If you are good and lucky, you get papers.

'Have you got any?' I asked Saker.

'I will have soon.'

'*Inshallah*, I will get them for you.'

There are limits to one's trust in Allah. So I asked Saker to row me in the dinghy down the creek to the Customs House, where I had made friends with a Customs officer and the assistant harbour master, Ali al Sakdoum. He was there in his white *dish-dash* and *aghal*. I explained about Saker and said

I wanted to hire him as a sailor for my dhow.

He looked him over. 'He is an illegal immigrant.'

'He *was* illegal!' I said.

Ali smiled and said, 'OK. We shall establish his identity.'

He could have enforced the law there and then by deporting Saker. Instead, he sat down at his desk to ask a few questions.

'Name?'

'Saker.'

'Surname?'

'Saker.'

'Where born?'

Saker looked up. I said 'Bombay.'

'Date?'

'1950,' I said.

'Day and month?'

I said without hesitation, 'May 11th.' (My birthday.)

'Son of?'

'An orphan ... a foundling.'

'Present address?'

'Dhow *Mir-El-Lah*,' I answered for him.

'Height?'

I grabbed Saker and pulled him to me. 'I am six feet. Put down five feet.'

Ali glanced down and wrote: 'Five feet.'

Then he told me, 'You must get two photographs and he shall put his thumbprint on them as well as on this paper.'

I took Saker to the nearest photomaton. Ten minutes later, Mr Saker Saker, Indian Able Bodied Seaman, legally existed and rowed me back to the *Mir-El-Lah*. I felt I had just adopted a child. He stayed with me until I left Dubai; he remained there to make some money and buy himself a wife. He said he could achieve that ambition by working hard for five to ten years. *Inshallah*, of course.

The world of the dhows is a man's world. I knew that many of the carpenters, like Kabul, were married, but I was never invited to meet their wives and hardly ever caught sight of them. Their women are treasured possessions, to be kept at home, hidden from the eyes of other men.

One evening Seif Mohammed handed me a letter addressed to 'Lorenzo, Behind the Bridge, Dubai.' It was from Muriel, a French girl I had met once before. She said she loved me and wanted to come and live with me while I worked on my dhow. I was lonely, so I wrote the single word 'Yes' on a tablet of teak and sent it to her care of the French Embassy.

Two days later Muriel moved into my tent. She was tall, with long chestnut hair, green eyes and big feet. She had disturbed her distinguished family by accidentally burning down a *château* on the Loire and had been exiled to Dubai to live with a cousin working for an oil company.

What a relief it was to have company! We played chess and backgammon under the Chinese hurricane lamp which swayed and cast weird shadows on the canvas. The sound of wind blowing sand against the tent made us feel we were at sea.

After her arrival the time passed quickly and soon the *Mir-El-Lah* was ready for launching. Seif Mohammed greased the baulks of timber so that she would slide smoothly. We removed the timbers that supported her upright, leaving her gently leaning on sandbags facing the creek. Kabul, hopping like a great bullfrog, slid beneath her, to slit the bags with his knife. The weight of her hull squashed the sand out of the bags until her keel rested on the greased baulks. For a moment, I was certain Kabul would be crushed to death, but he knew exactly how much time he had to escape from beneath her. It was a fascinating method of launching, as old as the dhows themselves. The only sign of the twentieth century was the appearance of two Bedford army trucks with car tyres fastened to their front bumpers. They reminded me of the tame elephants in Thailand, as they moved forward in low gear, pushing the *Mir-El-Lah* until she glided gently to meet the rising tide that would float her at high water.

We were about to cheer, Kabul was standing on the bulwark giving orders when the sixty-foot-long *boom* fastened to the mast came crashing down to strike him between the neck and shoulders, carrying him with it into the creek, where he lay face down in the shallow muddy water. We all feared he was dead.

We rescued him as quickly and gently as we could, but dared not move him far in case of internal injuries. Seif and I dashed to the hospital for a doctor, while Muriel stood by guarding him. When we returned Kabul was back on his feet talking to her. The doctor proclaimed him fit to be driven to the hospital.

Several factors saved his life: his great physical strength and powerful shoulders had resisted the blow; the *boom* had missed his skull by inches; and there was just sufficient water and mud in the creek to cushion his fall.

Once I was satisfied that Kabul was well cared for, I sent a telegram to Domenico Ravera in Khorramshahr, telling him the *Mir-El-Lah* was afloat; he took the next plane to Dubai.

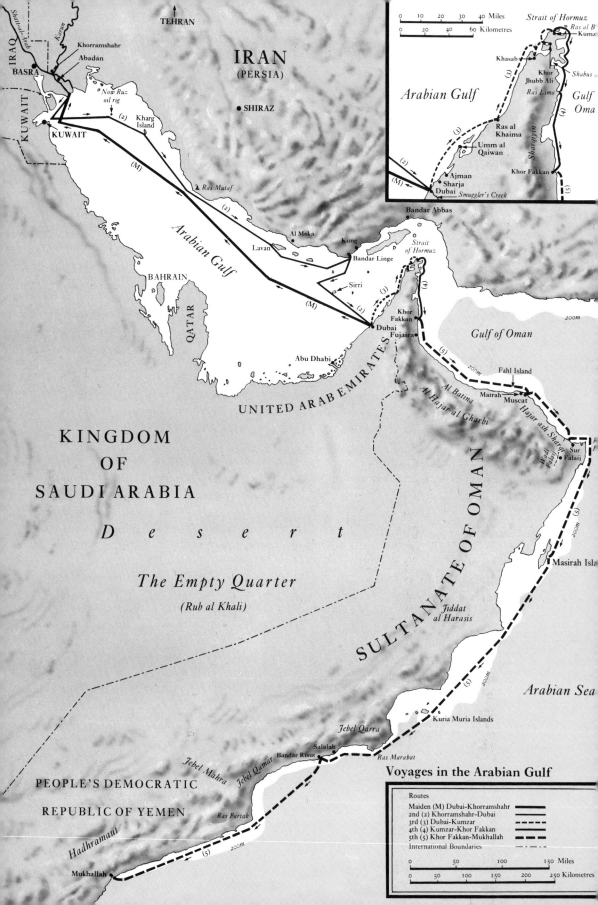

TEHRAN

IRAN
(PERSIA)

IRAQ

BASRA
Khorramshahr
Abadan
Now Ruz oil rig
Kharg Island

KUWAIT

SHIRAZ

(M)

Ras Mutaf

(2)

Arabian Gulf

BAHRAIN

Al Moka
Kung
Lavan
Bandar Linge

Sirri

QATAR

(M)

(2)

(3)

Bandar Abbas

Strait of Hormuz

Khor Fakkan
Dubai
Fujaira

Abu Dhabi

UNITED ARAB EMIRATES

(4)

Gulf of Oman

(5)

Al Batina

Al Hajar al Gharbi

Fahl Island

Matrah
Muscat

Hajar ash Sharqi

KINGDOM
OF
SAUDI ARABIA

Wadi Falaji

Sur
Falaji

Desert

The Empty Quarter
(Rub al Khali)

SULTANATE OF OMAN

Jiddat
al Harasis

200m

Masirah Isla

Arabian Sea

Kuria Muria Islands

Jebel Qarra

(5)

Bandar Risut
Salalah

Ras Marabat

Voyages in the Arabian Gulf

Jebel Mahra

Jebel Qamar

PEOPLE'S DEMOCRATIC

REPUBLIC OF YEMEN

Ras Fartak

Hadhramaut

(5)

200m

Mukhallah

Routes
Maiden (M) Dubai-Khorramshahr
2nd (2) Khorramshahr-Dubai
3rd (3) Dubai-Kumzar
4th (4) Kumzar-Khor Fakkan
5th (5) Khor Fakkan-Mukhallah
International Boundaries

0   50   100   150 Miles
0   50   100   150   200   250 Kilometres

Inset map:

0   10   20   30   40 Miles
0   20   40   60 Kilometres

Strait of Hormuz

Ras al B
Kumz

Arabian Gulf

Khasab

(3)

Khor
Jhubb Ali

Ras Lima

Shabus

Gulf
Oma

(3)

Ras al Khaima

Umm al Qaiwan

(2)

Ajman
Sharja
Dubai

(M)

Smuggler's Creek

Khor Fakkan

(5)

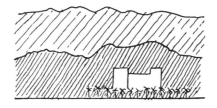

6. Maiden Voyage

We loaded up with water, fuel and stores and left Dubai flying the Panamanian flag, a flag of convenience in the truest meaning of the word. Indeed, in the circumstances it was the only flag I could fly. The *Mir-El-Lah* had been built in the Emirate of Ras-al-Khaima, towed unfinished into Dubai Creek where Abdul Rahim Godai had completed her and I had altered her to my own requirements. I am an Italian national, the dhow was sailing to Kenya, my home base. She was now on charter to Anglia Television, an English company. The *Mir-El-Lah* was the first dhow to be registered in Panama. Equally important to me and my Arab friends was that country's beautifully coloured star-spangled banner. It was immediately proclaimed throughout Dubai that I was a dependant of the 'Sultan of Panama'.

In the world of the dhows the name *Mir-El-Lah* became *Emir Allah* – 'God is King'. I had both versions inscribed on her bows, one in Western characters, the other in Arabic. Arabs are not fussy by nature, and nowhere was this difference ever disputed.

Domenico Ravera was in command as I was on my maiden voyage and had to learn as much as possible during this trial trip; it was a wonderful chance to sail with a professional sea captain by my side. With us came Muriel, Mohammed – the same Mohammed who had lost his father at sea – and another sailor called Ali, a black man from Sur whose origins I traced to Zanzibar. They had signed on for Khorramshahr, from where they would be flown back to Dubai.

We sailed at sunrise straight for Khorramshahr, seven hundred miles away at the head of the Gulf, from where we were to make the start of the classic dhow voyage to East Africa. The Dubai Creek, or Smugglers' Creek, has two pronounced bends in its last half-mile into the Gulf. It is very narrow, so it is hard for two vessels to pass each other on the curves. The superstructure of a large utility vessel steamed towards us, also flying the Panamanian flag – she greeted us with several blasts on her siren. I was steering and getting the feel of my beautiful new wheel. Domenico was giving orders navy fashion, and I asked him to use 'left' and 'right' as 'port' and 'starboard' still rattled me. Ali was at the controls below and I had to shout my orders to him down the hatch: I had at least learned that ahead meant forward, astern meant reverse, and stop meant STOP.

The *Mir-El-Lah*'s engine thumped regularly, and once we were out in the Gulf I gave the wheel to Muriel and pulled out my fishing kit. I tied a bright-yellow plastic squid with a good stout hook to a steel trace five feet long, with a swivel before a hundred feet of nylon line. I watched the squid jumping in our smooth wake: a good wake, I had been told, meant a well-built ship.

Ali and Mohammed prayed on deck, facing Mecca. They had unrolled their prayer rugs and stood looking straight ahead before dropping to their knees to touch the mats with their foreheads, taking their weight on the palms of their hands. They repeated this several times before sitting back on their haunches and gazing beyond the distant horizon. With one eye on the fishing line, I read the *Gulf Pilot*, checking for shoals and hazards in our course. Domenico took sights and bearings with his sextant and checked the beautiful compass he had presented to me. Muriel steered without over-correcting as most beginners do. We were all happy to be at sea and the sea seemed happy to receive us.

At ten o'clock at night I took my turn at the wheel. We were to leave the island of Sirri some twenty miles to our right – starboard. It was cold; I was wearing a sweater under an old black oilskin of Domenico's and wore the traditional red and white check turban round my head in the Omani fashion. A thin layer of cloud or mist darkened the usual brightness of the stars by which I was steering. The *Mir-El-Lah* was performing well – the ninety-horsepower Japanese Kubota engine, which we had thought might not be powerful enough, was giving us an estimated six knots at half-speed, and was not yet even run-in. It sounded healthy and its vibrations were minimal.

I had not yet got the hang of things and was very aware of my limitations, especially at night. It was like driving a car without lights, I thought. For hours I stared at the black wall around and ahead of me. The wind was light, but brought with it a long swell. I began to wonder if I was really alive and if the hands on the wheel were really mine.

Then I saw a strange light, low in the water. It was drawing closer, green and glowing; it seemed to cover a wide area. I altered course to avoid it. Muriel was sleeping behind me on a mattress spread on the deck. I shook her feet, waking her, and told her to come and look.

'What is it?' she asked, sitting up. 'A submarine? Or a monster?'

We were almost on top of it. I had seen phosphorescence before, but never like this. It was entirely different from what I had seen in Kenya or even in the South Pacific. Then I saw several neon-lit torpedoes, speeding straight for us. Fairy tale porpoises, magically lit green creatures, gigantic nocturnal glow-worms of the sea.

Muriel and I watched transfixed. I handed her the wheel and went to sit astride the bowsprit. Phosphorescence was also sparked by the ship's bows.

Hearing our excited chatter, Ali appeared on deck. He was not in the least puzzled by it: it was nothing new to him. We saw several such glows, some very near, some quite far off.

Dawn broke in lovely pastel colours. The sea was flat calm. Not a breath of wind. The sun rose. I was still riding the bowsprit and could see my reflection in the water below, as in a mirror, created by the shadow of the large bow and the angle of the sun.

On the fourth day we ran aground, in broad daylight! Near Ras Mutaf, a spit runs out for twenty-five miles, only a few feet beneath the surface of the water. We should have been to the north of the lighthouse that marked its northernmost point. The *Mir-El-Lah* suddenly lost speed, our wake turned to dark muddy brown. I rushed to the engine room, reduced speed and slammed her into reverse. Too late. We were stuck on a sandbank.

Mohammed took soundings with a long bamboo pole. We drew five to six feet. After a considerable struggle and a great deal of shouting we ploughed our way astern until we refloated and the colour of our wake changed from brown to green again. Domenico suggested we go south for half an hour, then east for two hours, before shaping north by north-east again.

That night the sun set unseen. Mountains of ragged clouds went down with it as if a giant whirlpool were sucking them under.

'There is a great wind,' Ali said.

'*Shamal*, much *shamal*,' added Mohammed.

We were a night and a day from *Now Ruz* – the 'New Year' – the northernmost Irani oil well of the Gulf. The *Now Ruz* with its ever-flaming gas flares marked the entrance to the Shatt-al-Arab. Our course was set to sight the red glow of the flares at about midnight.

Ali and Mohammed tied down every movable object. The big tarpaulin

Overleaf Dates are packed in round straw baskets and punted down canals to the waiting dhows in the Shatt-al-Arab

over the poop was secured with extra lashings, and several spare planks were used to strengthen the sides, for the *Mir-El-Lah* was not yet hardened to the sea and ready to face a storm. Like all dhows she was 'leaky', and even on the calmest days we had to pump out the bilge twice a day. Her decks had been caulked and tallow-fatted, but the scuppers were too small to carry away the water if we shipped a big sea. I was afraid her engine-room would certainly be flooded.

In less than an hour the wind rose. We caught fleeting sights of the moon as it appeared and vanished behind the low, racing clouds, like a witch's lantern in a forest. Ali worked hard at the hand pump, but such was the violence of the rising wind that not a drop from the pump's mouth went over the side. The filthy bilge water blew over us, drenching us and covering everything with stinking grease. I tied my pillow around the mouth of the pump and stopped the unwanted shower. By the time I finished the job the *Mir-El-Lah* was being struck by a heavy sea. She rose to it bravely and, as she plunged into its trough, her bows disappeared into a second and even larger sea.

This was, indeed, her christening. '*Ego te baptismo Mir-El-Lah in nomine Patri et Filii et Spiritus Sancti*,' I said, crossing myself, the infidel.

Ali and Mohammed worked with buckets, shovelling the incoming water towards the only two scuppers on either side of the poop. I had better save the engine and the electrics, I thought, and grabbing two blankets, while Muriel kept the hatch raised, I slid into the dark belly of the *Mir-El-Lah* where the blessed engine was still dry and thumping quietly. I flashed my torch and noticed the shaft under water, which meant we had to keep pumping all night. We could well have to face even bigger seas ahead.

I fixed the protecting blankets as best I could so that they did not touch the engine. The *Mir-El-Lah* bucked stoically through the waves. Suddenly a blinding flash followed by a cascade of sparks filled the engine room with thick acrid smoke. A short circuit. I smothered the sparks and flaming bits of plastic wiring-tape around the alternator and cursed myself for not dealing with it sooner. I felt suddenly sick. I switched off the batteries and came on deck, eyes streaming, half choked by the fumes.

Domenico was at the wheel; Mohammed was pumping; and Ali watched the night through Domenico's binoculars, wiping them frequently with the sleeves of his *dish-dash*. Nobody said anything. I was learning the unwritten laws of the sea. Do your own thing. Ali and Mohammed knew the dhow had to be pumped all night; they never questioned it. We all knew there was an element of risk involved; we also knew we could turn around, hoist our sail

Dubai: Pakistani dhows bring meat for the oil-rich Arabs. Goats
are notoriously bad sailors: this one was in a hurry to get off

and fly before the wind. Right now we could still keep our northerly course.

I saw no trace of apprehension in the faces of Domenico, Ali or Mohammed. They were men hardened to the sea and knew the rules of the game. I did not. I was as green as a pea.

'Your turn now!' Domenico shouted to me above the wind. 'Ease her over the waves – slice through them at an angle. Not too much, just a little.'

I had been watching him carefully and understood.

Ali went forward. He returned after a while. '*Now Ruz,*' he shouted at me, pointing to the east. I did not see a thing for an hour; and then I finally saw what he had detected so long before, a flickering liquid red glow.

'*Taijib,*' Ali said. 'Good!'

Mohammed went on pumping. Clunk. Clunk. Clunk. The wind was easing. Domenico was stretched out on a sodden mattress. He had seen the red glow too. '*Ci siamo,*' he said to me in Italian, 'we're there.' We would be at the estuary of the Shatt-al-Arab by daylight. It was a difficult channel with a great many sandbanks and a lot of traffic – not only dhows, but tankers as well.

The *shamal* died as quickly as it had risen. By daylight we were moving through a flat muddy sea, surrounded by distant lands. Iraq was on the left and Iran on the right. Ali pointed south and said, 'Kuwait.' I could see a line of vapour floating at sea level.

'Kuwait?'

'Yes, Kuwait, yes, yes! Kuwait, rich, rich!'

I followed the gaze of his pirate eyes, chasing a stream of gold, with greed but without hope.

'*Allah karim,*' I said.

'*Allah akbar,*' he echoed. And we had coffee.

We steamed up the river all day, amongst the date-palm groves that lined both banks of the Shatt. Dhows lay on the green sandy marshes, like whales left to rot in the sun; new dhows were being built. The canals that fed water to the date groves were busy with punting 'gondolas' laden with baskets of fruit.

We hoisted the Irani flag and kept to the right side of the river, demanding and expecting protection. There were sentries and gun emplacements on both sides. Near Khorramshahr the banks bristled with guns – machine-guns and anti-aircraft guns, dug-in tanks, radio and radar aerials. Hiding behind a bundle of sails I looked at this lethal display of hardware through my glasses. Those excitable, untrained soldiers had trigger-happy fingers. Better show a low profile, I thought, even if the *Mir-*

El-Lah is motoring up the waterway to the Terrestrial Paradise, the original Garden of Adam and Eve.

We dropped anchors in mid-stream; a motor launch was approaching us at speed. I cut the fuel and for the first time in several days we heard the sound of silence.

'I will do everything,' said Domenico. 'I know everybody here. Let me handle papers, passports, customs clearance and immigration formalities. You go home and tell Francesca to cook the four frozen partridges I shot last autumn.'

I did not then realise what a formidable task lay ahead of him. He told me afterwards he had 'offered his chest to the firing squad' if we turned out to be 'bad' people and that he himself, with his chest, would remain behind until everything had been settled to the satisfaction of the authorities. It took him three days to clear our empty dhow and fly Ali and Mohammed back to Dubai from Abadan. He came home only to dine and sleep, leaving early each morning, his briefcase bulging with papers.

I flew back to London a week later and Muriel went back to join her cousin in Dubai. The *Mir-El-Lah*, spruced up and well oiled, was still in midstream when I went aboard to say goodbye to her. The scalding hot summer was drawing near, when one feels the earth has slipped its cables and is drifting closer to the sun.

PART TWO

7. The Journey begins

In October Mirella and I left London for Iran. To travel with Mirella is a delight, for she has an eye for beauty and an enormous sense of fun. With her I see things I would not notice alone. Like a butterfly flitting from flower to flower, she passes from one vision to the next, leaving behind her a disorderly trail of cameras, films, filters and lenses that have to be retrieved from the curious and the predatory.

Despite the intense heat, we made our way through Iran by car; we visited the mosques and the bazaars of Shiraz. From here comes some of the merchandise that finds its way into the holds of the dhows when they sail to Africa. Shiraz, surrounded by mountains, was refreshingly cool. We walked our feet sore in the labyrinth of streets and through the legendary covered main bazaar, cool and dark after the bright hot light outside. The clattering sounds of the streets were strangely subdued; here everything seemed to hum. Even the people looked different; they did not hurry, they seemed to glide. All the beautiful handmade products of Iran were on show. Carpets of every size, colour and price were piled in great heaps spread on the floors and hanging from beams. There were baskets and earthenware pots, hand-printed materials with mysterious ochre and brown designs, hand-woven woollen shawls of maroon, red, green and yellow, astrakhan hats, and great fluffy sheepskin coats as deftly embroidered as the matching silks. There were also plastic suitcases and tin pans, plastic shoes and cheap mirrors, combs and perfumes. Piles of sticky syrupy sweets and cakes made from honey, covered in flies, lay on great silver platters. And carpets, more carpets, carpets everywhere.

For some time we had heard loud clanging noises, and as we moved further into the bazaar the noise became deafening. We found ourselves in the copper alley, which stretched for about half a mile. Lined on both sides with stores like small grottoes, it was very dark and covered all over with a sooty dust. Red-hot burners spat out sparks that fell and died in the blackness of the interior. Little skeleton men worked like galley slaves bent over the flames, beating their creations with shattering hammer-blows. Dressed in filthy torn shorts, their emaciated bodies and faces were covered in the same grey dust that hung in the air and clung to the walls. Their hollow eyes stared at us from sweat-streaked faces. Mirella and I watched transfixed as the copper sheets spun through their hands with incredible speed and dexterity and turned into the fat-bellied water-containers with gracefully curved handles, the long slim vases and the beautifully moulded trays piled all around them. When we asked about the price, smooth sleeky-dressed vendors with brilliantined hair rushed up and called for the scales. What we chose was weighed and sold by the kilo. The hard work and artistry of the little men sweating over their burners seemed to be taken into little consideration, if any at all.

While we wandered through the bazaar we noticed certain women who stood out from the others. They were much taller, with straight noses, high cheekbones, dark sunbaked skins and arrogant strides. They wore long, voluminous, brightly coloured, gathered skirts that swished from side to side as they walked. They wore no veils and looked us straight in the face with black piercing eyes. They were the Qashqa'i nomads who wander across the plains and mountains of Iran twice a year, driving their herds of camels and sheep from the winter to the summer pastures. They were also the weavers of the beautiful Qashqa'i carpets we had seen on the dhows in Mombasa and in the bazaars.

Later on our five-hundred-mile journey to Abadan we came across them again; a long trail of brown, curly haired camels moved slowly beside them, their elegant long necks and drowsy heads swaying in rhythm to their nonchalant gait. At sunset they pitched their tents, which looked like great black cobwebs hanging from sticks planted firmly in the ground. When it was time to move on, they were neatly folded, rolled and tied to the backs of the camels. The women and children piled on to the backs of horses, their skirts covering the horses' hindquarters almost to the ground. They looked like Spanish señoritas on their way to a fiesta.

The caravan with its hundreds of black-and-white long-haired sheep, its camels and horses, moved no faster than the most overladen donkey. Oblivious of the traffic, the nomads ignored the shouts, curses and klaxons of the frenzied drivers – the meeting of two worlds, each trying to assert its right of way. For Mirella and me it put the clock back centuries and we travelled slowly in their company for a while.

As we drove through the night we followed the flames that shot hundreds of feet into the blackness from the oil wells. The earth belched her gases into the air as man harnessed the endless flow of black oil pouring from her guts. We arrived in Abadan at midday and at Khorramshahr, our destination, half an hour later. The oppressive heat made us sweat profusely. Mirella stood it better than I, perhaps because of her African childhood. The sudden switch from our oven-like car to Domenico's air-conditioned villa proved too much for me. When I woke the next morning I felt as numb as if I had spent the night in a refrigerator.

At breakfast, when I questioned Domenico about my dhow, he told me she was nearly ready. His carpenters, Abdul Faz and Ari, had been working on her for six months. Pleased by this news, I proposed visiting her that afternoon. I had forgotten about the stifling heat now that I had grown accustomed to the air-conditioning; I had also forgotten my friend's incurable optimism.

As we passed through the main gates to the harbour, we were halted by a guard who looked suspiciously at Domenico's diplomatic plates; he touched the car as if it were a mirage. He was joined by a more important guard, with one star on his tunic. They stared at us like angry bulls. A man with two stars appeared, followed by another with three stars, who returned to the gatehouse only to come back with yet another with four stars. This last one escorted Domenico back to the gatehouse for a conference that went on for a very long time. Meanwhile Mirella and I baked in the back seat of the car.

Finally, permission was granted for us to proceed. We drove through a familiar maze of old tyres, broken crates, rusting cars and smashed machinery. Ice-boxes and air-conditioning plants, corroded with salt, stood in long lines as if awaiting the firing squad. Armed soldiers lurked behind them, rifles at the ready, lest we attempt to pillage such treasures. We raced along the wharf until it petered out into a sand track at the water's edge.

'We've arrived!' Domenico shouted triumphantly.

The first thing I noticed as I got out was the squashed body of a rat we had run over, its tail still twitching. Carcases comprised much of the flotsam in that oil-polluted harbour.

Then I saw my *Mir-El-Lah*. She was lying on her side in the stinking shallow water; an umbilical cord of narrow planks supported on rickety

Overleaf The Qashqa'i migration. Some of the carpets
they weave end up in the holds of the dhows

wooden stilts attached her to the shore over mud and marsh some fifty yards away. The large white tarpaulin that had provided the shade on deck and poop was brown and hung in tatters, lacerated by weeks of *shamal*. Her planking had opened up, dried and split by the blazing heat of the summer sun. A dead cow, its belly bloated, its legs stretched heavenward, bobbed against her bows. The stench was appalling.

I just stood there staring, forgetful of the midday heat, like someone who turns up at a funeral too late.

Domenico's voice broke the spell. 'She's beautiful, isn't she? A bit dusty, but we'll soon clean her up. The planks are split here and there – they just need a bit of caulking. Linseed oil will turn her into the best-looking dhow in the Gulf.'

I thought of the last time I had seen her, anchored in mid-stream, her well-oiled woodwork shining gold in the setting sun, the white tarpaulin stretched tight and securely lashed to the mast.

I looked at Mirella. The expression on her face reflected my feelings.

'The show must go on,' I whispered to her.

'Follow me,' Domenico called to us, as he set off over the swaying planks like a tightrope walker. 'If it bears me, you two are safe enough!'

Even while he spoke I heard a sharp crack as the plank supporting him collapsed, depositing him up to his waist in mud.

Mirella and I stared down at him, trying not to laugh as he struggled out. He had lost his *espadrilles*, but was quite unperturbed as he took off his trousers, rinsed them in the dirty river water, wrung them out and put them on again. He was a man not easily discouraged.

He borrowed a little aluminium dinghy and climbed into it. Using a broken plank he paddled out to the *Mir-El-Lah*. I climbed aboard, pulling Mirella after me lest she too ended up in the reeking cesspool. I felt some flickers of hope. Six sweltering months in this hell-hole would have killed any other vessel, but not the *Mir-El-Lah*.

Then Mirella turned to me. 'Lorenzo, there's no way! We'll never make it in time. Not for at least another month.'

'The wind does not wait,' I retorted. 'If we miss the north-east monsoon we can't possibly hope to reach Africa.'

I was still too upset by all I had seen to argue with her within earshot of Domenico. So I led Mirella forward and said, 'Go home, darling. I'm sorry. Either I'm terribly right or terribly wrong. But, as I don't know, I'd better face this on my own. Please go home! I'll get to Mombasa somehow.'

I saw her start to say something, probably something kind and to the point, but I did not hear her voice. Then I lost sight of her. Her face suddenly became indistinct and out of focus.

When I woke up I was in a hospital bed. I had a violent headache, my tongue seemed too big for my mouth, my fingers tingled. I saw Mirella at the end of my bed. She was asleep. I looked at her and waited for her to wake, but I must have fallen asleep once more.

When I awoke again, everyone was in the room. Mirella, Domenico and his wife Francesca, her granddaughter Raffaella, as well as a doctor, a nurse, and the carpenters Abdul Faz and Ari. They were talking in hushed voices – I heard them saying I had heat stroke. Then Mirella came over to me and, taking my hand, told me how, when we were talking on deck, I had suddenly collapsed. My eyes were open and my pulse was very faint. She had been terrified, convinced I was dying. But the irrepressible Domenico had reassured her.

In three days I was on my feet again; I recovered sooner than the doctor had expected. As soon as I could take the sun, Mirella and I set about the mammoth task of repairing our dhow. We hired more carpenters and sail-makers and threw ourselves into the work. The fact that we had a deadline to keep urged us on.

But in spite of all our efforts I knew the *Mir-El-Lah* would never be completely ready in time. All that really mattered was that she should be seaworthy, her planking watertight, sails strong, compass correct, engine and electrics in running order. Creature comforts I left to Mirella and Domenico. My determination was mainly motivated by lack of confidence in myself, for I kept asking myself whether I was capable of handling the dhow, always wondering if I was not completely crazy to attempt it. Perhaps my greatest fear was sailing at night. It seemed to me unbelievable that I could dare to navigate my dhow in unknown waters and darkness with only a compass, the stars, a chart and occasional sightings of shore lights to use as guides.

'You have to watch out for the tankers at night,' Domenico told me, with his Mona Lisa smile. 'They travel at twenty knots, they can be anything up to three hundred yards long and displace as much as three-quarters of a million tons. When a tanker sights you – if she does – and alters course, she has already covered several miles. A dhow is little more than a piece of driftwood to a tanker, and if she hits you she won't even feel the bump!'

'Then what the hell do I do if I meet one? Change course?' I asked.

'Good God, no! If you are on course and have the right of way, carry on. Remember, if you both change course you will almost certainly have a collision. That's what happened to the *Andrea Doria* and the *Kungsholm*,' he recalled.

'But how do I know when I am on the right course and have the right of way, or whatever you call it?' I questioned naïvely.

'That's simple. Check your navigation lights with hers. Remember the doggerel – "Green to green, and red to red, hold your course and go ahead".'

'How far off can I see her lights?' I asked with rising apprehension.

'That depends on the weather and visibility. Sometimes it's not so easy,' he answered.

'How often is sometimes?'

Domenico shrugged. 'About sixty per cent of the time. But don't worry; it'll be all right. What is tricky is when you have several other ships around you. Then you have to work it out. But you are a *nakhoda* now and that is only one of your problems. Maybe you should fit a radar or a reflector screen: small wooden vessels don't show up well on the tankers' radars.'

November 15th. I awoke in a good mood and decided to sail that evening – *Inshallah!* If I had not named my dhow after Mirella I would have called her '*Inshallah*'. I wrote out our itinerary and fixed it to the mast.

> '*The sambuk* Mir-El-Lah *sails tonight to East Africa via Abadan, Arabian Gulf ports, Dubai, Khasab, Khor Fakkan, Muscat, Sur, Ras-al-Hadd, Masira, Salalah, Mukhallah, Ras Hafun, Mogadishu, Lamu, Kilifi and Mombasa. Inshallah.*'

I decided to sail at night because darkness above all would hide my fears. I also planned to arrive at the estuary during daylight. New problems would then begin: shifting *maraqqat* (soft sandbanks), incoming and outgoing traffic, ocean-going steamers and tankers.

We left Khorramshahr on time and with a new crew, Ahmed and Shaiyad, chosen by Domenico, and the voyage began. Definitely a twentieth-century voyage, with deadlines to be kept and engagements to be met, a trip during which a film was to be made. Yet, without such a programme and pressures, the trip would never have been undertaken.

I was following in Sinbad's wake, but not at his pace. My powerful diesel engine was there to propel me when Sinbad's sails would have hung limp, waiting for the wind. A necessary compromise. No wind – start the engine. No sleep – take a pill. How clever we are today; we think we have all the answers!

From the Karun we entered the Shatt-al-Arab and turned left towards

Abadan, only a few miles away. On both sides of the river I could see clearly the flickering lights dotting the date groves. Charcoal fires and hurricane lanterns hanging outside the huts of the date farmers and harvesters, tiny fragments of the world of dhows.

My dream was slowly coming true. I was now one of those thousand Sinbads who had sailed this way south to the East African coast. I tried to think with Sinbad's mind to return to his simplicity. It was important to find out if this was still possible. Could it have been this which drew me to the sea and into this adventure?

Inevitably, from the outset I had repeatedly asked myself if I would be capable of making the voyage without the engine. It was tempting to find the answer by switching it off and trying to make the Gulf with the winds, the tides and the currents. Even if I had had the time, would my brain and nervous system endure the slowing down such a voyage would require?

As I watched the lights onshore, I longed to meet the people living in those huts, to share their lives, know their names and learn about their families and their dreams. I was taking but a superficial glance into their world, attempting to film a life which was disappearing as fast as I was trying to capture it with the camera.

An acrid smell of burning rubber and frying grease brought me back to reality. Smoke seeped through the cabin ports. I yelled to Ahmed to slow down and take the wheel.

I traced the smoke to the poop cabin beneath the floorboards.

'Stop!' I yelled to Ahmed. 'Stop!'

While Ahmed dropped anchor, I lifted the floorboards and found the engine shaft bearings red hot. It would only have been a matter of minutes before a fire started; but as soon as I switched off the engine the smoke began to clear and only the black grease around the shaft, slowly turning blue, continued to sizzle.

My incompetence as a mechanic is matched only by my total ignorance of engineering principles. Mechanical failure had always been one of my worst fears. Now we needed outside help, for not one of us had a clue about repairing the shaft. *Allah karim! Allah akbar!*

Once the engine had been silenced and we lay peacefully at anchor twenty yards from the Irani shore, an almost magical change seemed to take place. The tall date palms whispered in the night breeze, the plovers called, the new planking creaked as it adjusted itself to the teak frames. We were out of time again. Now I began to feel that this voyage would give me what I was searching for – between film engagements and countless problems, Mirella and I would catch a glimpse of the world of the dhows. And with such hopes I fell asleep.

Next morning we flagged down one of the many utility tugs that ply between the Shatt-al-Arab and the oil rigs. The *Artiglio* was owned by an Italian friend of mine from Khorramshahr and was on charter to Agip, the Italian oil company. The engineer came aboard to look at the shaft. His name was Frederick. Small, round and white like a piece of garlic, he lived almost entirely in his engine-room where, he said, he drank more beer than his engines drank fuel. Highly paid and happy, he told me, he would soon be able to afford to return to his native Austria and buy a farm. After inspecting the shaft he came back on deck, wiping his hands with cotton waste, and grabbed the glass of beer I offered him.

'Your shaft is out of alignment,' he explained. 'The heat of last summer has dried the wood and the engine has sunk on to its seating at least one inch. Hell of a job! The shaft is bent and needs straightening.' Seeing the look of horror on my face, he slapped me on the back. 'Don't worry. It's only a bit of metal and no bit of metal should sadden a lucky fellow like you with such a beautiful wife!' he chuckled, waving his glass towards Mirella and slopping the beer on deck. 'I shall fix it for you. It will only be a temporary job, but it will take you to Dubai.'

The following evening, and a case of beer later, we restarted our down-river trip. In spite of Frederick's reassurances I was more apprehensive than ever. Mirella and I kept sniffing the air. Many times the scent of the fires burning on the river banks or the stench of the oil from Abadan threw us into panic and sent us dashing to the engine-room. Abadan, once the world's greatest oil refinery, is now obsolete – its rusting cranes hang like cobwebs in a haunted house, abandoned steel barges litter its shore. The word 'pollution' must have been invented for Abadan.

South of the port the river flows more swiftly as it widens, and countless fishing canoes seemed hell-bent on committing suicide across our bows. Ahmed explained that they were fishermen whose only chance to set their nets across the river is in between the stream of passing craft. As soon as they sight an approaching vessel, they must haul the nets in before they are cut to ribbons.

When the moon set at about four in the morning, we hung a hurricane lamp from the bows so that the fishermen could see us in time. I reduced speed to the minimum and sent Ahmed forward. He was proud of his eyesight. He looked like a kestrel with his sharp, beak-like nose. From the wheel, I could discern his ghost-like shape crouching by the bowsprit; now and again he raised his right or left arm, indicating my change of course.

The dawn was not far off. I smelt it before I saw it.

Suddenly I felt a slight thud against our side and saw Ahmed peering into the water. He came aft.

'*Allah akbar,*' I said. 'What is it?'

Ahmed loves me when I praise God; he begged me never to say 'goddammit', as I often did.

'*Allah karim,*' came the inevitable reply.

We heard a voice, an unfamiliar voice; not Mirella's or Shaiyad's. Listening, we heard it again. It did not come from below deck. Ahmed went to the rail again and let out a torrent of guttural sounds, waving his arms for me to stop the engine.

I pushed the gears into neutral and joined Ahmed and Shaiyad, who had come up on deck from the forward cabin, bringing a torch with him. We looked overboard into the terrified face of an Arab boy in a canoe.

Somehow a rope trailing from the canoe had become entangled in our rudder and we had been towing him ever since I had heard the thud against our side. Fearing some awful punishment he had kept silent until, even more frightened of being towed miles from home, he had started moaning and praying. Vociferating something to the wretched lad that had a lot to do with Allah's infinite mercy, Ahmed lowered a knife to him on a line. The fear died from his eyes as he cut himself free. We watched him drift astern in our wake as the dawn broke around us.

The tangle of black shadows faded as one by one the date palms were silhouetted against the pale-blue sky. Hundreds of wildfowl winged their way eastward, greeting the rising sun with their cries. The Shatt-al-Arab, wider at this point, was now mahogany brown like the distant mountains of Dashistan and Tangistan. The sun was black as it rose over the estuary; I had never seen it look like that before and wondered if it foretold a storm. But as we left the last of the date groves behind and reached the muddy marshlands, it burst from its shell and flooded the sky with its orange light.

Soon we were in company – attractive company. From the side canals and villages came a small fleet of river dhows, so heavily laden with fresh green grass that their hulls were scarcely visible. Together we moved towards a little Irani destroyer anchored in midstream with several dhows moored alongside her. When her crew spotted our Panamanian flag, they began shouting their heads off to make room for us. But it was not until an officer, armed with a pistol and looking like a dried fig in a wig, jumped aboard followed by six sailors that I realised it was not a friendly welcome.

Pointing his pistol vaguely in the direction of my head, he shouted abuse at Ahmed in Parsee. Pausing for breath, he turned to his men for support. They shook their heads like marionettes, making it clear that they were behind him. I felt like asking Ahmed when we would face the firing squad but, fearing the joke would remain untranslated, I produced the stack of documents I had collected from the Imperial Navy of Iran, the Savak, and the Customs and Immigration officers of Khorramshahr, impressively decorated with fifty-four different stamps.

The dried fig brushed the precious papers aside with contempt and, accompanied by two sailors, made for the cabin. I dashed after him, fearing one of them might steal Mirella's cameras. But I was too late. Immediately he saw the cameras the fig's expression registered suspicion and triumph. Every camera was brought on deck and laid out on the engine hatch.

We were surrounded by grass-laden dhows and dozens of Sinbads of all ages gaping down at us, titillated by the sight of an unveiled woman and eager to witness the next act of the drama. Delighted by such an appreciative audience, the fig stood up to deliver a long passionate oration.

I asked Ahmed to tell me what he was saying.

'Very bad, very bad ... spies we ... enemy, Iran, Shainsha bum-bum war ...' he answered, racking his limited English for hostile words.

There were at least thirty dhows alongside the destroyer, all straining on their anchors; we were a green island in the barren estuary. I was growing gradually more nervous, for in such situations there is no telling how long they may keep you or what may result. After watching the Irani officer cleaning his nails with a knife until I could bear it no longer, I again produced my documents, together with our passports. He glanced at them and waved them away.

'Khorramshahr,' he said. Suddenly it dawned on me that he could not read and, fearing punishment from his superiors and humiliation before his men, he was ordering us back whence we had come.

I was boiling with rage, conscious of the Bofors gun trained on us from the gunboat's deck. I decided to try bribing him. Suddenly the situation resolved itself as the dried fig shrieked and covered his face with his hands.

Mirella had pointed a camera at our tormentor. Leaping to his side, I put an arm round his shoulder and asked Mirella to take our photograph. The ruse worked. Vanity overcame stupidity. He shouted to one of the sailors to bring his cap, his leather belt and a sub-machine-gun.

When Mirella had finished her roll of film, she opened the camera and gave him the spool, she pointed at me, at the sail and the southern expanse of the Gulf. After a long silence, during which we held our breath, the dried fig consented to let us go. Thanking him profusely, we kissed our hands, touched our foreheads and our hearts, and as soon as he and his sailors left we hauled our warps and pushed our way through the grass canyon.

For the first time on this voyage I opened the *Gulf Pilot* for guidance. On page 295 it read as follows:

> *'The Outer Bar Reach is approached through Khawr al Amaya, a narrow gut leading north-westward from the Shatt-al-Arab light-vessel past Kafka Light Buoy. The axis of the outer part of this channel is indicated by a pair of leading lights, etc., etc.'*

The trouble was I never saw the light-vessel or Kafka Light Buoy, or any other beacon mentioned in the *Pilot*.

I was in the middle of a vast expanse of muddy water with high peaks fading into clouds and nothingness in the south-east. Dozens of fishing craft dotted the estuary; a freighter was heading towards me making for a conical red buoy, no mention of which was made in the *Pilot*. My only concern was to let this vessel pass, and when I clearly saw she would steam to the right of the buoy I sailed to the left, assuming that as long as I was close enough to the buoy I could not possibly go aground.

Despite my inner resistance to calculations and nautical terms I grew to love the *Pilot* with its related charts. Together with my compass it became my constant companion. But with my disorderly mind I was never able to master that book's intricate instructions. In any case it had been overtaken by the rapid march of time. Leading landmarks such as the minarets of mosques, forts and even mountain peaks were now lost amidst high-rise buildings and vast oil refineries, and the beams of lighthouses and beacons were dimmed by the eternal flames of the countless oil wells. Despite this the book became for me not only a necessary source of vital information, but also a source of great amusement. It also taught me never to jump to conclusions, never to assume that what appears to be Cape Fartak really *is* Cape Fartak. One faulty assumption by an amateur navigator can lead to many others. I was never entirely convinced that I was on the right course or in the right place, and was, therefore, never entirely right or wrong.

8. The Gulf

Once in the Gulf, we headed south-east under power towards Bushire, an Iranian port a hundred and twenty miles from the estuary of the Shatt-al-Arab. The sea was calm and the *shargi*, a suffocatingly hot sticky wind from the south, made it impossible to hoist the lateen sail to spare the engine shaft, which was smoking again. Although this was not enough to make it seize up, I improvised a cooling system with the aid of a rubber hose through which we poured water on to the hot bearing case and shaft.

Night fell quickly. My second night alone as a *nakhoda*, responsible for the *Mir-El-Lah* and all on board her. I no longer had experts like Domenico to whom I could turn for counsel. I was determined to keep my fears to myself and prove to Ahmed and Shaiyad that I had the situation under control. Between us there had developed a strange understanding. They were far more knowledgeable in the ways of the sea and of ships than I and had taught me much. Now, however, it was up to me to show them they could sometimes trust me.

Kuwait was on our right, and dead ahead in the distance lay the *Now Ruz*; the glow of the oil flares in the darkness comforted me and gave me a great deal of confidence. Between us and Bushire lay Kharg Island, Iran's most important oil terminal, twelve miles long and, according to the chart, marked by no fewer than twelve lights. Out of bounds to all unauthorised shipping, Kharg is under constant patrol by sea and air and has a gigantic radar station. Its approaches are divided into two lanes for incoming and outgoing tankers. Everyone in Khorramshahr, including my friend the Admiral, had painted an alarming picture of Kharg Island for me, so at least I was not unprepared for the hazards ahead.

When Ahmed pointed into the darkness and called, 'Tanker, Captain,' (which he pronounced 'Capen'), I calmly looked through my binoculars and, turning the wheel over to him, said, 'She's yours now,' and sat down to have a mug of tea. But under my breath I kept repeating 'green to green and red to red' as I tried to judge our distance, speed and course, finally satisfying myself that the giant tanker was bound for Kuwait and would pass well astern of us. By studying the chart and checking my watch frequently, I hoped to reassure Ahmed that the *Mir-El-Lah* was safe in my hands. I flashed my torch on to the chart and indicated to him that the tanker was bound for Kuwait. From that moment on I was the *nakhoda*.

Soon after midnight I sent Ahmed to bed so that he would be fresh when he took over his spell at the wheel at dawn. I myself was dangerously drowsy and had to sing to keep awake. I discovered that if I altered my course the *Mir-El-Lah* made different sounds that immediately alerted me. How quickly the senses adapted themselves to these sounds! I felt the slightest shift of the wind through the hairs in my ears, or realised I was off course because one side of my nose got colder! I also found out on that second night at the wheel that it was easier to steer by picking one star than by keeping my eyes glued to the quivering compass-needle.

Frederick, the engineer of the *Artiglio*, had told me that I would 'hop from flare to flare' and now I understood what he meant, for I felt like a moth being drawn to those irresistible flames lighting the horizon at Kharg Island.

I know of no better place for dreaming and talking to myself than at the wheel of a dhow at night. And that night as I watched the distant red flares I was never more conscious of the changing world in which I lived.

When I had first planned my trip to the Arabian Gulf and the Arab Peninsula, I had had to look at an atlas for the whereabouts of Abu Dhabi, Dubai, Ras-al-Khaima, and Sharjah, so unimportant and remote were they. Just as I began making my first discoveries, the oil crisis exploded and the world press was full of my secret names. I felt as if the treasure I had so painstakingly been trying to uncover had been accidentally unearthed by some bulldozer.

Page 167 of the *Gulf Pilot* made me smile: 'Landing on the mainland between Dubai and Abu Dhabi is not recommended, for it is often visited by Bedu from the interior.' I imagined Mirella sold to some lecherous, paunchy, camel-riding sheikh, myself being buried up to my neck in sand, a mug of water before my eyes and honey smeared on my forehead to attract ants and flies, as I died slowly and painfully in the blazing sun.

Again I was brought back to reality by the acrid smell of burning rubber. I dived below and checked the main shaft. No smell. No smoke. It was rotating gently at half speed. When I returned on deck, black smoke was rising from the engine hatch as if the *Mir-El-Lah* were some old tramp steamer that had lost a funnel.

Shouting to Ahmed and Shaiyad, I dived below again. Mirella's anxious face appeared. 'What is it? What's the matter? I can smell burning.'

'I'll let you know in a minute. Don't worry,' I told her.

While Ahmed opened the hatches and ports, Shaiyad filled two buckets with salt water. (I was told later that this was the last thing one should do in case of fire.)

I was driven on deck by the thick black smoke; I switched off the engine by cutting the fuel supply.

'Don't worry.' I smiled bravely at Mirella and decided those two words should be carved in wood and stuck up everywhere for future reference.

When the smoke cleared we returned to the engine-room to find that the cooling pump had broken down and the engine had dangerously overheated.

For the first time in my life I had to repair an engine on my own. I spread a canvas mat on the floorboards to avoid the contents of the water-pump running into the bilge, and unscrewed the first of four bolts holding a large main plate down. The first three were easily removed but the fourth refused to budge. I tapped it with a hammer, covered it in penetrating oil, and tried to wrench it free with a spanner, but only succeeded in breaking off the nut. Undaunted, I prised the main plate off with a screwdriver. Six tiny coils sprang from it in all directions. Not one fell on my mat. One landed in Shaiyad's turban, but it took a good hour of desperate searching to find the others. Those springs, I learned later, were housed in the middle of six rubber washers. It was pointless trying to replace them as four of the washers had disintegrated and the other two came to pieces in my hand.

As with the wooden engine seating, the summer heat had played hell with the engine itself. Now it was dead – or, if not dead, completely unconscious. There was nothing left to do but hoist the lateen sail.

Despite the almost superhuman effort required, Ahmed and Shaiyad went about it with savage joy, chanting their dhow songs, for they hated the engine – it was smelly, unreliable and hostile. The great lateen sail was our saviour and we raised it with loving devotion. We might as well have hoisted our bedsheets to dry. The sail – it has been said before – 'hung limp'. Our souls hung limp. My face hung limp. There was no wind.

I opened the emergency box for the flares and rockets I had bought from Captain Watt's Albemarle Street store in London, still unable to believe I was about to launch a rocket into the night sky. Yet we did need help.

I turned, as always when in doubt, to the *Gulf Pilot*. It told me on page 20 that the south-westerly wind can be followed by the *shamal* within an hour or so. This change is often extremely abrupt. On January 10th, 1950, HMS *Mauritius* experienced a violent squall when the wind changed almost instantaneously from south-south-west, seven knots, to west-north-west, thirty knots.

Comforted by this information, I decided to use three parachute rockets at half-hourly intervals. Before doing so, I referred once more to the *Gulf Pilot*, knowing that while we drifted we were at the mercy of the currents. Currents north of *Now Ruz* were very weak. So the rockets were our only hope of rescue before the *shamal* struck.

After reading the instructions and following them to the letter, I uncapped the rocket, held it aloft with a trembling arm and nervously pulled the trigger, expecting my head to be blown off.

The rocket shot up and up and then exploded with a sharp crack, the little red light hanging from the parachute as it slowly descended, giving the men on the rig time to see it.

'Let's have *chai*,' I called to Mirella. 'They'll be coming out to us soon.'

She quickly produced cups of hot tea, along with some biscuits from Khorramshahr which, like the washers on the water-pump, distintegrated on contact.

Ahmed, Shaiyad and myself sat by the mast watching for tell-tale signs of the approaching *shamal*; we passed the binoculars to one another and scanned the *Now Ruz* where we could just see the lights on the rig platform'.

'There are probably two dozen men on that platform,' I said, in a feeble attempt to keep up our morale. 'That makes forty-eight young eyes'.

Half an hour went by, and I fired the second rocket. When, another half-hour later, I fired the third and last rocket, I decided all those eyes were closed tight and that, had we been sinking in a raging storm, my rockets would have only lit up one more sea tragedy.

I read the instructions for handling the hand flares. They were to be held as far away from the face and eyes as possible until they burned out. I have long arms and decided to light the first one myself. As soon as I had done so I felt both my face and hand burning. I yelled to Ahmed to bring me a pair of pliers. When I saw him running towards me with a hammer I almost threw the flare at his flowing *dish-dash*. But then Shaiyad was behind him with the blessed pliers and in seconds I had the flare at a safe distance. By the time it had burned out, my right arm smelt like Kentucky fried chicken and I decided that next time somebody else could play the Statue of Liberty!

Five minutes later, I spotted green and red lights racing towards us from the *Now Ruz*, and I shouted to Mirella that we were being rescued. She made more tea.

A tug pulled alongside the *Mir-El-Lah*; the helmsman radioed to the rig that we were not on fire as they had thought, but had engine trouble, that we were Italians, and he requested permission to take us in tow to the rig.

His name was Giovanni Bellori and he was from Ravenna, currently working for the Italian oil company leasing the *Now Ruz* from the Irani Government. So, he explained with a grin, we would not go short of *pasta*. He told me that they had seen our rockets, but as there were many smugglers armed with machine-guns in the area they had decided to wait for further distress signals before taking action. From a distance they had mistaken my burning flare for a ship on fire.

Giovanni told us once more of the tight security surrounding all oil rigs, and that we would have to undergo extensive screening and interrogation. A helicopter was already on its way from the mainland with a general from the Savak and the chief engineer of the area. But I told him exactly why we were there and assured him he had nothing to worry about – we had more documents and permits than we could possibly need.

'*Ma siete un po' matti voi, no!*' he exclaimed, '*e poi la sua bella signora cosa ci fa' in mezzo a questo schifo di mare?*' ('You're crazy. What is your lovely wife doing in this stinking sea?') He was certain Mirella and I were mad to be sailing around the Arabian Gulf in an old dhow.

By then, we were between the gas flares and the oil rig itself.

After climbing up over a hundred slippery steel rungs to the main platform we were greeted by a trio of Italian technicians, especially glad to see Mirella. '*Ben' arrivati!*' they shouted. '*Prego signora, gradisce un caffe' espresso?*' ('Welcome! Would you like an *espresso*?')

'You are the first beautiful lady to come aboard.'

Now that we were safe we were able to laugh at what was happening. We had just been rescued from possible disaster, we were having *espresso* and *panettone Motta*, on a forbidden oil rig which had to be the first landmark in our exploration of the world of dhows. We told them our story and they told us theirs. They were happy to see we had enough papers to justify our presence on their rig. Otherwise, they said, '*Un sacco di storie ...*' ('a lot of problems').

The sun was rising when we heard the helicopter approaching. The jet-ranger flew in from the north-east and landed effortlessly on the platform. Two men and the pilot climbed down, shaking hands all round before drinking more *espresso*.

The general from Savak was a fierce-looking tartar who spoke no English. The Irani engineer was good-looking, a dark-haired Valentino who spoke fluent Italian; he kissed Mirella's hand before we sat down in the control-room. He told us we would not have to show our papers; they had already contacted Tehran and Khorramshahr and our credentials had been checked.

When I explained what was wrong with our engine and showed them the remains of the washers, Giovanni was called in. He studied the washers briefly and said, 'We cannot make these here. We need Teflon and we only have it at the base.'

The handsome engineer turned to the general, and explained the situation in Parsee. The general nodded and smiled, clearly in agreement with all that was being said. Giovanni was instructed to fly to the mainland in the jet-ranger, make the new washers in duplicate, and return to us within six hours.

We were entertained to a wonderful lunch that would have done credit to Maxim's, Prunier's or Alfredo's; the menu included caviare and oysters, and French and Italian wines.

Within four hours Giovanni was back. Placing the washers on the table, he said proudly, 'Your engine won't go wrong with these.' Then, bending down, he whispered, 'If you had to buy these, each one would cost you one hundred dollars!'

We left the rig at six that evening. The general shook my hand and warned me through his interpreter, 'Whatever happens, stay away from Kharg Island.'

Back on board the *Mir-El-Lah* everything went smoothly. We dined off a ten-pound mackerel we hauled in and, although the engine was ticking over perfectly, we took advantage of the north-easterly breeze and hoisted the sail, making such good speed that I reckoned we would sight Bushire by four the following morning. To guide us we kept the flares of the *Now Ruz* astern and in the distance, on our left, those of Kharg Island.

But at midnight, just as I was handing over the wheel to Shaiyad so that I could get some sleep, we smelt burning again. Trusting Giovanni completely I did not even attempt to open the pump, guessing correctly that a different set of washers had disintegrated. I switched off the engine, in the knowledge that once it had cooled down I would be able to use it intermittently in an emergency.

We had to sail until the engine cooled. The fresh breeze carried us nearer and nearer to Kharg Island. By tea-time the following afternoon we could see clearly the steel towers, antennae, smoke stacks and a forest of grey masts. When we approached the first of the oil rigs I hoisted my Panamanian flag, the Irani courtesy flag and the yellow flag which I hoped they would recognise as a request for a friendly inspection.

The men on the rig waved to us as casually as if they were millionaires at a seaside restaurant who had spotted a party of yachting friends. I waved back. So much for the efficiency of their security. Jets flew over our heads, helicopters skimmed the water a few yards away. None of them paid any attention to us; I remember Domenico telling me that radar could not detect wooden vessels. We were surrounded by rigs and tankers, and with the diving gear I had aboard I could have slipped over the side to attach limpet bombs to any of them. Clearly these technocrats had come to place so much trust in their gadgetry that they did not bother to use their eyes!

The sun went down and was replaced by an artificial Aurora Borealis made up of oil flares, searchlights, intermittent flashes, ships' lights and navigation lights. The reddish-brown hills of Kharg Island, the rigs and the tankers were lit like a movie set.

We were no more than a mile off-shore – it was nine o'clock and no one had yet come near us. Without bothering to lower the sail I switched on the engine and followed the jagged coastline until I found a suitably sheltered anchorage I dropped a hook and went to bed.

Just before sunrise we were awakened by bugle calls, roaring engines and the high-pitched whine of helicopters. They've finally caught us, I thought. But no – they were just the normal morning sounds of Kharg. Back on deck I noticed that we had anchored in what appeared to be the very heart of the military installations of the Island. To our left, alongside the inner pier, lay several naval vessels, ranging from PT boats to destroyers. On our right an airfield was bursting with activity – on the water's edge helicopters were warming up their engines, and jeeps and hundreds of soldiers were swarming about like ants. Phantom jets traced smoke circles in the sky. Just ahead was a little village of barracks and what seemed to be a whole battalion of soldiers standing stiffly to attention as the flag of Iran rose slowly to the truck of a tall white flagpole. Away at sea the superstructures of several tankers and the sprouting steel towers and rigs with their flares burned palely in the morning sun.

It still remained a mystery to me why not one of those Samurais housed, fed and paid to guard this island against intruders had raised the alarm. We were so blatantly out of place, anchored right beneath their noses, that now I wanted them to see us, even capture us, if for no other reason than to find a mechanic to fix the water-pump. If the mountain would not go to Mohammed, Mohammed would go to the mountain.

I rowed ashore in our dinghy, determined to appeal to the naval authorities rather than to the army: the former might be more sympathetic towards a seaman in distress! Making fast the pram astern of one of the destroyers, I climbed on to the pier, gathered a few astonished looks, and made my way up to the most imposing building where I hoped to find some intelligence – or intelligent – officer who might help me.

At the gates the might of the Imperial Irani Navy, in the person of an armed sentry, barred my way.

'Good morning,' I greeted him, brandishing my documents. 'Could I speak to your Commanding Officer?'

He stared at me in blank astonishment. But when I repeated my question I only succeeded in making his thick black moustache tremble.

Soon we were joined by an officer in white who looked equally surprised to see me. Once again I had to take the initiative.

'Good morning, sir! I am in command of the Panamanian dhow *Mir-El-Lah*,' (I longed to add 'And I demand your unconditional surrender'), 'and my water-pump has broken down.' I said. This sounded so ridiculous that I had to struggle not to laugh!

It was obvious that it did not matter in the least what I said, for he looked from me to the dhow, did an about-turn and disappeared.

The element of surprise is invaluable, I thought.

A telephone rang, then another. Sentries shook themselves from their torpor. Several men in blue overalls raced towards a PT boat and I knew they would be heading for the *Mir-El-Lah*.

An armed guard beckoned me to follow him and led me into an upstairs room where five officers stood waiting.

I felt like saying, 'Please, gentlemen, be seated,' but refrained and repeated my friendly 'Good morning.'

They continued to stare at me for several minutes and I expected one of them to open my mouth and check my teeth. The element of surprise was fading. They sat down and offered me a chair.

Since none of them chose to ask it, I recounted my story from Tehran to Kharg and laid my documents on the desk.

The senior officer examined them, passed them to another officer and asked in impeccable French, '*Vous parlez français?*'

'*Oui, assez bien, mon commandant.*'

Relieved at being able to talk to me he pointed out that I had broken the tightest security regulations in the whole of the Arabian Gulf.

I tried to explain that I was well aware that I was guilty of trespass, but only because my pump had packed up and I had been blown into Kharg by the *shamal*.

The three telephones on the desk kept ringing. But they were drowned by the noise of a small motorcade arriving – a signal for the officer to turn round

Overleaf In the Elburz Mountains in Iran. We set off from Tehran and reached the Caspian Sea two weeks later

on me and announce, 'You are under arrest!'

'What about my pump?' I demanded.

I got no answer; the door was flung open and an Admiral swept into the office, looked me over, addressed the others and then dismissed them so that we were alone.

'You have acted most foolishly,' he rebuked in English, so that I felt like a schoolboy facing his headmaster.

'But my pump ...' I began.

'Your pump!' he laughed, cutting me short. 'Mr Ricciardi, you should have broken your pump elsewhere. You should never have come near Kharg, putting yourself in this most unfortunate position and causing us so much trouble. I know it is not your fault, but ...'

A telephone call interrupted him, giving me time to collect my wits. The man was right. What the hell was I doing even in the vicinity of Kharg? Why had I not made for Kuwait instead? It was all Marco Polo's fault, I told myself. He, too, had sailed from Khorramshahr in his dhow and, romantic fool that I am, I was determined to follow in his wake along the southern coast of Persia. But then again, why had the Iranis chosen the damned island as the headquarters for their oil game? I could not be blamed for that either. Nor could I be blamed for the fact that they had failed to detect the *Mir-El-Lah*. That, in fact, was the crux of the whole affair, and it strengthened my position. It was the Admiral who was getting it in the neck. And that was all too clear from his crestfallen expression as he put down the telephone.

'Mr Ricciardi,' he said, almost pleadingly, 'please go away and stay away. We will repair your pump at once. But please leave. I will have a gunboat to escort you from the prohibited area.'

I could have retorted that I needed no escort as I knew the way, but he was kind and I felt sorry for him.

For the next few hours the best mechanical brains in the Imperial Irani Navy worked on my pump. The four extra washers Giovanni had made were fitted to it, the engine was started, the water flowed from the exhaust-pipe; and, as the anchor was raised, the mechanics jumped over the side into the PT boat.

We left Kharg Island at about mid-day. Well past the three-mile limit, the PT boat escorting us increased speed, lifted its bows and sailed off, leaving us on our own again.

9. The Greeks

After studying the chart I decided to change course – instead of heading for Bushire I would take Marco Polo's route for Jazireh-ye-Lavan, two hundred and fifty miles from Kharg. No wind, however strong, could carry me back that far into trouble! In Lavan I would find old friends from the Cornuti Club – the Cuckolds' Club: fantastic food and clear water in which to swim and dive. I might also find some pearl fishermen, and Mirella could get to work with her cameras.

I discovered that on this new course we would have to pass the shifting sands of Ras Mutaf, where we had run aground the previous year on our passage from Dubai to Khorramshahr; so I plotted our course well clear of the light that, according to the *Gulf Pilot*, marked the limit of the sands. I calculated we would sight this leading mark at noon the next day, and sure enough we did! Mirella was most impressed!

Although there was little wind, we hoisted sail and kept the engine running. We were out of the shipping lanes and had a peaceful night.

By morning the wind had freshened considerably, and after a consultation with Ahmed and Shaiyad we agreed to stop the engine – voluntarily this time – and sail to Lavan. No sooner had we done so than the wind died and we were becalmed.

When I pressed the starter nothing happened. We checked the battery leads, cleaned them, greased them. No luck, the batteries were dead flat. I tried to recharge them – our battery charger would not start. It needed a spare part obtainable easily in Paris. We were adrift once more!

At about six in the evening we sighted a mastless dhow under power. Frantically we waved bedsheets, and Mirella waved her *kikoi* from the deck. The crew of the dhow waved back some rags and sailed right past us.

We sighted another vessel. I ordered our sail to be lowered. As soon as she was near enough I would light a flare. Through the binoculars I saw to my astonishment that she was a shrimper from Galveston, Texas. What could she be doing ten thousand miles from home in the Arabian Gulf?

As she approached and slowed down I saw two Europeans scanning us through their glasses. Drawing alongside, the two swarthy men, looking

Overleaf Fishing nets to be lowered near the *Dara* wreck off Ras-al-Khaima

around them suspiciously as if fearing attack, clambered aboard. They were Greeks, Spiro Stavroupolos and Cristo Panayotis. Spiro, acting as spokesman, introduced himself and his companion.

'Our battery is flat and we need a tow,' I told him.

'So! I can get you started with my battery,' he replied, moving to the engine-room, followed by Cristo.

They returned on deck looking depressed. There was nothing they could do, Spiro announced: the starter motor was also faulty.

'Then take us in tow,' I proposed hopefully.

Spiro looked even more disgruntled as he poured out his tale of woe.

'Trouble – nothing but goddam trouble!' he wailed, rolling his big black eyes heavenwards. 'Trouble with the Persians, the Arabs, the American Fifth Fleet, even the bastard Turks!'

On and on he went. Why should they help us, if no one helped them? We could be spies, smugglers. We were more trouble – more big, big trouble.

All the while the two men eyed Mirella's legs lecherously. Feigning tears, she gave them a watery smile. Spiro's manner softened. 'Women are all troubles! But don't cry, lady.'

I suggested they should tow us back to their mother ship, for by then I had gathered they worked for the Ross Kalachekis fleet of shrimpers.

'The boss will blow his top!' moaned Spiro. 'We will never hear the end of it. What's in this for us?'

'Money,' I replied.

He sniffed contemptuously. 'Money – we have more money than we can spend! You are trouble for me – big trouble. Come aboard and have coffee.'

In the shrimper's cabin, while Cristo called his mother ship on the radio, Spiro made thick black coffee and as he handed a cup to Mirella nearly poured its boiling contents over her breasts.

After Cristo had ended what seemed an interminable row over the radio, he said, 'Now we must go to the mother ship and take orders from the boss.'

'Are you coming back or not?' I demanded, trying to look tough.

'I come back – I come back in four-five hours. OK?' he answered.

Taking Spiro aside, I lied dramatically, 'Come back for my woman – she is pregnant.'

We returned to the *Mir-El-Lah* and I went below to sleep for a few hours. If they had not returned by midnight I would use our flares again. We had only a dozen left and I was running out of SOS devices. As usual, with difficult problems to face, I slept heavily.

I was awakened by Ahmed shaking me and telling me a ship was heading for us. By the time I was fully awake I felt the *Mir-El-Lah* shudder, her timbers creaking in protest, as she moved forward with a sudden, violent jerk. Spiro had returned earlier than expected and had wasted no time in taking us in tow at such an alarming speed that I was certain my poor dhow would disintegrate under the strain. I tried without success to signal to him to reduce speed. This, I thought, must be the ultimate test. If the *Mir-El-Lah* could survive this tug-of-war, she would prove herself the strongest wooden vessel still afloat.

Some hours later I picked up the bulky shape of the mother ship through my binoculars. She was surrounded by thirty or more shrimpers bobbing in the swell. She reminded me of a fat sow suckling her litter of piglets. The moment we were made fast to one of the trawlers Cristo and Spiro abandoned us and, as they jumped from shrimper to shrimper to the mother ship, I could still hear Spiro chanting, 'Trouble – trouble – nothing but trouble!'

Then a voice called, 'Hey, you! Yes, you, Capitan – *buon giorno amigo!*'

I recognised the tall, hugely fat man standing on the deck of the shrimper next to us holding a bucket full of shrimps as Aris the Greek from the Airline Hotel's restaurant in Dubai.

'Aris, *amigo*, come aboard and drink with us. It is good to see you again!'

With an agility amazing for a man who must have weighed at least two hundred pounds, he climbed to our deck without spilling a single shrimp from his bucket. He handed it to Mirella, who immediately dropped it, scattering the shrimps, alive and kicking, all over the deck.

Shrieking gulls swooped down for the feast. Roaring with laughter, his great belly heaving, Aris shouted above the din to Mirella, 'Good morning, lady. They are good – very good. Don't give them all to the birds!' Driving off the gulls, he retrieved the bucket and most of the shrimps. 'Grill them, grill them on charcoal. If you don't have any, I have. Then put some olive oil on them. If you don't have any, I have. And squeeze lemon over them. If you don't have any, I have. And with them drink a litre of Aketeopoulos wine. If you don't have any, well ...' Looking sheepish, he scratched his chin. 'Well, I think I have finished mine.'

His expression soon changed when Mirella put a beer into his hand. Settling his vast backside on the bulwarks, he looked around him. 'So you have your dhow. That night in Dubai I remember you tell me you look for a *sambuk*, but you have no money. I hear all the time people saying they want to buy a dhow, they want to do this and they want to do that, but then I never see them again. But you – you are different! I see you and you have your dhow and you are at sea with your wife, and this is why I meet you,

Overleaf Sheikh Mohammed-al-Maktum of Dubai. He took us to the desert in his helicopter where we hunted *habaras* (lesser bustard) with hawks

because me and all these people here, we are all sea people. I will make life easy for you here now. Spiro is my greatest friend, but he is also the most stupid man I know. All the time he grumble. I know his wife; she is from Santorini. Don't ever marry a woman from Santorini! Go off with one, if you like, but after a little, run away from her because those women make you crazy. I know because my wife is also from Santorini. That is why we are shrimpers so we are away from them. Far away. Too much, too much, my friend!' Sighing deeply. Aris emptied the beer in one gulp.

When, to my surprise, Spiro came back, Aris upbraided him for taking us for spies or smugglers. 'Lorenzo he is my good friend from Dubai,' he told the sulking Spiro. And to prove the point, I produced more beer.

Ignoring Spiro, Aris turned to Mirella and me. 'You see,' he explained, 'I am a big father here. All these are my children. When they go to sea I count them and I count them when they come back. If they are not all here, I will look for them. Sometimes, the *shamal* blow very strong like the *meltemi* in Greece.'

'You are wrong,' Spiro interrupted. 'You are not the boss. Mr Thermidos is ...'

Aris shut him up. 'He won't be back until next week, so now I am the boss. You go call Takis and he fixes this engine so my friends can leave.'

When we were alone, I asked, 'What's the matter with him? Why is he so afraid?'

'He is afraid of going to prison. You cannot blame him, because he has been in prison for ten years, in Turkey,' Aris told me. 'He was a smuggler – cigarettes, tobacco, whisky. Turkish prisons are very bad and Irani prisons are also very bad, but for a Greek the worst is in Turkey. So, please, you must understand him. He understands only shrimps. When he sees shrimps he is happy. If he sees anything else, he fears to go to prison.'

I broke open some good Italian wine I had been saving for just such an occasion, and for two hours we exchanged stories about Greece, Italy, France, Kenya and every country that had a coastline, until Takis appeared, accompanied by Spiro, who looked relieved and almost relaxed now that all responsibility had been lifted from his shoulders. Lighting a cigarette and accepting another bottle of beer, he picked a fat shrimp from the bucket, squashed it in the middle and tossed it to a flying gull.

'They are big this year,' he smiled and lapsed into silence.

I joined Takis in the engine-room while Ahmed peered down at us through the hatch, clearly determined to learn the mysteries of engineering. Takis was a good engineer; I watched his every move as he worked on the engine, finally declaring the starter as good as new. He blamed the usual things: rainwater, condensation and rusted contacts. Dhows, he said, were leaky craft. When the engine started without any trouble, he said, 'Great engine. One of the best. They never go wrong. It is the stupid little gadgets, like starters and batteries and water-pumps and bearings that go wrong!'

I could not see what difference it made, since those 'stupid little gadgets' stop the engine anyway.

When the time came to leave these people and their floating world I was reluctant to go. In the few hours I had spent in their company, especially Aris's, so many memories had been revived of eternal Greece, bustling Piraeus, the islands of Corfu and Crete. I could even have lingered in the company of Spiro and Cristo and their flotilla of Galveston shrimpers to learn more of their lives.

'Thank you, friends,' I said, giving them a few bottles of *chianti*. 'Drink to the people of the dhow tonight.'

Once under way I laid off my course for Lavan and opened my *Gulf Pilot*. It told me that Jazireh-ye-Lavan is brown in colour and low-lying except for elevations of about thirty-seven metres. The island, being only one mile wide and fourteen miles long, is exceedingly difficult to distinguish at night or in hazy weather. However, there was a single conspicuous tree in the centre of the island.

I need have had no fears, for I scarcely had to glance at the compass as I steered for the all-too-familiar oil flares ahead. In all fairness to the *Pilot* we did spot that tree. In the distance it seemed to be standing all by itself in the middle of the sea, but then the elevations appeared and finally the whole island underneath.

We moored alongside one of the cement piers of the new harbour being built at the southern end of the island, not far from a number of small dhows unloading their cargoes of vegetables, probably from Mugan or Al Moqham on the mainland.

The water was crystal clear and swarming with garfish. Mirella was anxious to go ashore to meet the famous members of the Cornuti Club, but I could not resist setting up my rod and line. The garfish is one of the most sporting fish on light tackle that exists. No sooner had my small strip of squid hit the water than a huge garfish, three feet long, took it and a splendid battle ensued. It leaped and raced away on its tail for fifty yards. I played it on my light trout-line until it tired and I brought it aboard.

After this exciting interlude, which provided us with a meal for our crew,

Overleaf Tea-time in the desert: trackers and falconers rest after the hunt

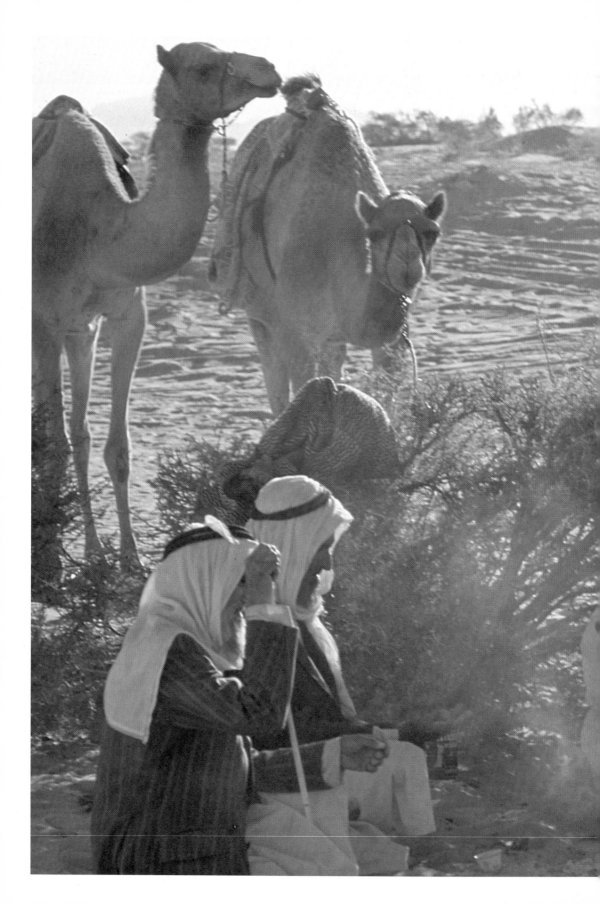

we set off for the Italian kitchens of Green Park, where the cooks were happy to see me again and overjoyed to meet Mirella. They tried their best to make us give up our trip and stay with them indefinitely. And, to convince us we were fools to leave, they served us an unforgettable meal: raw ham from Parma, cooked ham from Bologna, smoked hams from Friuli, salami from everywhere; parmesan on everything, *ravioli, fettucine,* fish mayonnaise, oysters, *agnolotti, fidellini, pastina in brodo, ragu ai tartufi,* and every kind of cheese invented by man. I felt guilty as I asked myself, 'Is this the world of dhows? Did Marco Polo feast like this when he landed in Lavan or did he content himself with old mutton chops à la Sheikh Soy'eb?'

Gastronomically our visit was successful but it was disappointing as far as the dhows were concerned, for Mirella and I had hoped to catch a glimpse of the elusive pearl fishermen known to visit the island. We had heard so much about their long, narrow dhows rowed by fifteen or sixteen men just as the galley slaves had rowed the triremes of ancient Rome. But we only found piles of empty oyster-shells scattered over the eastern beach. The few remaining fishermen left in the Gulf since Japan's cultured-pearl industry had robbed them of their livelihood had returned to their villages, while the rest had found better jobs with the oil companies.

On the evening of the second day we sailed for Bandar Linge, cheered on our way by a host of Italian cooks.

I had hoped to find this harbour slightly more lively than when I had last seen it for, after all, the season was approaching and by now the dhow people should have come out of their long hibernation to prepare for their passage to Africa. But once again I was disappointed. There were, it is true, three magnificent ocean-going *booms* in the harbour, their well-oiled hulls gleaming in the morning sun. But they were empty and not yet ready to sail. The town was as desolate as ever: the same debris everywhere, the same crumbling houses, the same overpowering stench.

I had almost made up my mind to leave without even going ashore when we saw an Irani Arab paddling towards us in a little canoe.

'*Jambo, Jambo, Karibu!*' he shouted.

'*Jambo, habari?*' we both shouted back. ('Hullo, what news?').

He was Mohammed-al-Fudain, whom we had last met in Mombasa the previous year, the *sekoni* – mate – of a large Irani *boom,* the *El Mansur.*

'*Mzuri sana, habari ya Mombasa?*' he asked, coming aboard. ('Fine. What news of Mombasa?'). Then he greeted Mirella, myself, Ahmed and Shaiyad in the traditional Arab fashion: '*Salaam aleikum.*'

'*Aleikum salaam,*' I replied, as always.

Like all citizens of the world of the dhows he spoke both Arabic and Swahili, so we conversed in the latter, while Ahmed and Shaiyad listened intently, nodding their heads with growing excitement as they recognised such familiar names as Dubai, Khorramshahr, Ras-al-Bab, Muscat, Mukhallah, Lamu and Mombasa.

Mohammed confirmed what I had already been told, that Bandar Linge, so often levelled by earthquakes, was an abandoned port. He lived with his family in Kung, only a few miles away, he told us, and Kung was the home port of the ocean-going dhows. There dhows were still being built. Everything was better in Kung: better men, better dhows, better houses. And, since it was only a few miles to the south, he invited us to come with him there the following day, so that we could see it for ourselves.

'But isn't Kung affected by these earthquakes?' I asked.

Mohammed was just about to answer when we heard a strange drumming noise that seemed to reverberate through the *Mir-El-Lah*'s hull as if someone were beating a giant tom-tom. On and on it went as we stood aghast, looking wildly about us. Then we saw that our aluminium pram dinghy, well lashed to the deck between the mast and the bulwarks, was shaking madly. We advanced on it cautiously, Ahmed and Shaiyad calling upon Allah. Wedged between the dinghy and the dhow's side lay a huge kingfish, its great tail fin lashing with all the strength of its thirty-seven pounds behind it. It had leaped from the water on to our deck. Even Mohammed in all his thirty years at sea had never seen such a thing happen.

Our dinner had fallen into our laps and who could be thanked but Allah, the Great and the Merciful?

The next day we went with Mohammed to Kung where, according to him, existed the oldest and largest colony of Irani Arabs.

It should be explained here that the greater part of the population of Iran is made up of people who, although Moslems, are not Arabs. They deeply resent any implication that they are in any way related to the Arabs, to the point that the Irani Arabs were almost considered second-class citizens. Mohammed went on to explain that the compulsory military service had done much to integrate them with the up-country Iranis and to lessen frictions between them. The Irani Arabs of Kung are still part of the world of the dhows, as they have been for generations, because they have found in the ocean the self-respect and peace denied to them at home.

Now, as we drove in our taxi to Kung, Mohammed described to me with such feeling the hardships of his people that I could no longer dismiss Bandar Linge as an eyesore. I was impressed by the efforts of its people to make a new life amongst its ruins, abandoning what was irreparable, strengthening what remained standing, constructing arcades from the rubble. Needless to say, Bandar Linge was not on the Thomas Cook list of tourist attractions, but once one knew its tragic history it was impossible not to admire its people.

We followed the road to Bandar Abbas, turning right at a pile of charred truck-tyres. Beyond them there was no road the driver could follow, and after risking getting stuck in the sand we decided to leave the taxi and continue on foot. In single file we marched across the sand dunes expecting to catch sight of the sea as we topped each crest, but found only an unending vista of undulating dunes. After half an hour's hard slogging we sighted the wind-towers of Kung. I felt that Kung was not on Irani soil, but was an independent, marine republic separated from the rest of the world by sands and sea. Finally, from the summit of the last dune we saw Kung, the sea and the dhows. A scene of utter desolation again met our eyes, the collection of wretched mud huts, the beach strewn with rotting fish, a bloated dead camel, the carrion crows feasting off its putrid flesh, an unfinished dhow, its bare ribs whitening in the sun. Mirella stood silent beside me; she did not lift her camera to her eyes.

We crossed the beach to the dhow and Mohammed patted its rudder, repeating, '*Taijib, taijib*,' 'very good, very good'. He was a devout Moslem; what Allah wanted to finish would be finished, what he wanted to be abandoned would be abandoned. I, being a bloody *mzungu* – a white man – could not share his philosophy; I wanted to save this dhow's life, take it away to sea, own two dhows instead of one.

As if sensing my mood, Mohammed pointed seawards where some two dozen dhows rode at anchor. 'In one month we go,' he said. 'Now it is still hot and everyone is sleeping.'

Our presence had been noticed through cracked walls and the peepholes of shutters, and soon men came running from their mud huts – fifty or sixty Sinbads – to greet us in Swahili. Amongst them I recognised my old friend Rashid, the proud little *nakhoda* of the *El Mansur*.

After asking their permission Mirella began taking photographs of the men. Rashid, without a trace of sadness, told me *El Mansur* had made her last voyage to Africa. She had been going there every year since his father's father had built her on this same beach, but now the African trading days were over. Too much paperwork, he explained, too many problems with the Customs in Kenya and Tanzania. No trade in Somalia. There was now only a small profit to be made picking up cargoes of *boriti* poles in Lamu, and half the fleet sailed there anyway. He himself had found a new and more profitable trade route, shipping flowering plants, potted plants and seeds to the barren gardens of the oil-rich Arabs of Dubai, Abu Dhabi and Kuwait. Others like him had discovered an equally lucrative business feeding and ferrying the hundreds of legal and illegal immigrants who were to build the Arab cities and the roads linking them so that the camel caravans could be replaced by the Mercedes and the Toyotas. 'It is good to sail where there is money,' he said. And when I told him that Iran had enough oil to be rich in its own right he shrugged his shoulders. 'Are we Irani?' he asked me. 'My country is my dhow,' he said.

The heat had become unbearable – we could not escape it by going into the houses where their women were. Mirella could, but by doing so she might create a problem with the other man of the house. So we told our friends we had a taxi waiting and must leave. Bowing their heads and pressing their hands to their hearts, they wished us a good journey and walked back across the beach, their white *dish-dashes* and headpieces floating behind them like tiny sails drifting over a sea of sand.

Mohammed was the last to go and, before doing so, he gave us a package of dates for his cousin in Mombasa, as if Africa was just round the corner.

Kung was nothing more than a convenient anchorage, a haven where the dhow people of Iran kept their women and children and spent their lethargic summers waiting for the action brought by the winds – an Arab enclave in an inhospitable territory.

10. The Storm

We sailed at dawn. I set a course for Sirri Island where we could anchor and spend a day. We had been underway for less than an hour when I first sensed that the weather was changing. The water was dark blue and the air struck crisp and cold. Ahmed sensed it too. He raised a wet finger to the wind and glanced up at the mares' tails overhead. '*Shamal*,' he said.

I hoisted the small storm-jib to steady the dhow in the rising swell and steered due west for Sirri with the *shamal* on my right. The *Mir-El-Lah* rolled heavily; the wind was freshening, the sea rising rapidly. There was no doubt we were in for a rough passage. After studying the chart, I decided to alter course due north heading into the *shamal* and the seas – under power I would then turn, hoist the mainsail and run before the wind for Sirri. My chief fear was that by doing this we would arrive after dark, and as there was only one guiding light, known to be unreliable, there was a danger of running aground. In fact, there were far worse problems I might have to face than that. In retrospect, I would be terrified to find myself in such a situation again, with no radio, no life-jackets, and only a tiny pram dinghy just capable of holding two people in a flat calm. It seems incredible now, but I had not given a moment's thought to the question of ballast. The *Mir-El-Lah* should have had ten tons. If ever there was a case of 'ignorance is bliss', it was that night.

We had to remove the canvas awning covering the poop before the dhow would take off like a kite. We managed after a considerable struggle, thanks mainly to Ahmed. God knows what I would have done without that precious Sinbad. From the moment he had raised his finger to the wind and the *shamal* had started humming in the shrouds, he seemed as one transfigured, as if the grace of Allah had descended upon him. There was no fear in his eyes, only rising excitement. Each time the bows of my blessed *sambuk* lifted to a wave and crashed back into its trough, he wiped the spray from his face and grinned gleefully back at me, his fierce black eyes drunk with the ecstasy of the possessed. Many times that night I had to borrow his smile.

By mid-afternoon, despite the rough conditions, we had made good time on our northerly course. Now it was time to face the greatest challenge of all: the hoisting of the lateen mainsail, a job that normally required eight strong men. Could the three of us manage it? And, if we did, would that enormous spread of canvas stay in one piece when I bore up and the *shamal* struck it at gale force?

I handed the wheel to Mirella. 'For God's sake, keep her head to wind!' I warned. 'Don't let her fall off. Please.'

To complicate things further, we had to shift the sixty-foot boom to the other side of the mast. This alone would have discouraged a lesser man than Ahmed, but he never stopped grinning. Every time we paused for breath, he shouted, '*Shamal! Shamal!*' as if defying the challenging wind.

By the time we had shifted and secured the boom I was so exhausted I almost decided we were unable to hoist the lateen. But a second look at the chart showed clearly it was now or never.

'Ready, Capen.'

Ahmed, Shaiyad and I braced ourselves, laid back on the great manilla halyard and started hauling with all our strength. The two men began chanting. I joined in, mumbling Arabic sounds with them.

I glanced over my shoulder at Mirella. She looked petrified, soaked to the skin, water dripping from her hair.

The boom was now halfway up the mast and the noise of the sail flailing in the wind was enough to panic anyone. It even silenced Ahmed as I dashed aft to reassure Mirella.

'Don't worry. Everything is all right. In a few minutes we'll be home and dry,' I said, hugging her.

What seemed like hours later, the sail was up, and as Ahmed made fast the halyards, I took the wheel. The position of the boom left me no choice but to bear away to starboard – or to the right, as I still called it. But for a few terrible seconds my hands froze on the spokes.

'*Turn*, Capen, turn!'

There was no mistaking the urgency in Ahmed's voice as he yelled at me.

Half-blinded by the spray, I leaned on the wheel with all my strength. The *Mir-El-Lah* hung stubbornly, not responding as she wallowed almost on her beam ends to port. I was certain we were going to capsize as she buried her gunwale under. Then, suddenly, I felt the wheel straining in my grasp and her bows swung to starboard, the *shamal* filled the great sail and we flew before the wind. At last, the *Mir-El-Lah*, rolling slightly, made use of her shallow draught and, without ballast, we must have been travelling at about twelve knots.

Towards evening we sighted a small white dot in the distance which we assumed was the light of Sirri. Passing it to starboard, according to the *Gulf Pilot* we were approaching what appeared to be a natural harbour. The good book warned that 'the anchorage off Sirri is difficult and the holding ground bad'. But we were too elated by the *Mir-El-Lah*'s performance on the run to Sirri to be depressed by such information, and as soon as we had rounded the point we set about the formidable task of lowering the mainsail.

The *shamal* was still blowing strongly, so that to this day I do not know how we managed to lower, furl and lash down the sail before it was blown overboard by a sudden, violent gust. Once it was down, we headed in under power into a blinding sandstorm that reduced visibility to a few yards. Following the *Gulf Pilot*'s instructions, I edged the *Mir-El-Lah* to within about thirty metres of the sandy shore and dropped both anchors. Amazingly they seemed to hold, but I took no chances and instituted watches. Ahmed volunteered to take the first. I went below and, like Saint Paul, prayed for the dawn! Ahmed and Shaiyad raised their arms to heaven, thanking Allah for guiding us through the storm.

Next morning the deck was inches deep in sand. It had penetrated everywhere – into our bunks, our food, our water, our hair, our mouths and nostrils. To protect ourselves we disappeared into sleeping-bags, leaving only our eyes uncovered. Later, dressed in *dish-dashes* and turbans we wandered like a ghostly quartet over the miniature sand dunes on the *Mir-El-Lah*'s deck.

The wind had eased gradually during the night: though we could still see the great angry white horses beyond our sheltered anchorage, we could also see through the veil of fine, driving sand that the sky was blue and the ragged clouds of the previous day were now white wisps, chased by the *shamal*. Heartened by such signs, I decided to make use of the wind to carry us on running free to Dubai, instead of waiting for it to die down.

I switched on the engine. It started! Ahmed and Shaiyad unlashed the sail, Mirella, looking out to sea, said, 'We have visitors.'

The *Austin Prince*, a large tug, was lumbering towards us from the east.

As she dropped anchor astern of us, I saw a man waving a red baseball cap.

'Could it be Domenico Ravera?' I asked Mirella.

'Yes, it's Domenico!' she answered delightedly.

With considerable difficulty a boat was lowered.

'God, I'm glad we've found you! We've been worried about you and searching for you all night,' Domenico told us as he climbed aboard and embraced us, full of emotion. He went on to tell us that the gale we had so miraculously weathered had been one of the worst for many years, rising to over forty knots at its peak. Several vessels had sunk, many oil rigs been damaged. Only sixty miles from Sirri a tanker bound for Dubai had capsized. Domenico had radioed Lavan, Bandar Abbas and Bandar Linge. Through the Admiral in Khorramshahr and his agent in Linge, he had been able to figure out that we were on our way to Dubai when the storm broke.

The *Austin Prince* had just arrived from Corpus Christi, Texas, and was bound for Jazirath Farur to salvage an oil rig that had broken adrift in the previous day's gale.

'I managed to talk her skipper into stopping at Sirri just in case you had made it. If we hadn't found you, we were planning to launch a full-scale search by air. But how the devil did you make it?' he asked.

I answered that we had hoisted sail and flown before the storm. Without Ahmed and Shaiyad, whom he had found for me, we would never have made it, I told him.

'You were lucky not to have a radio,' he said. 'Had you been listening to it you would have been scared out of your wits!'

'Beginner's luck!' I laughed.

He looked with envy round the *Mir-El-Lah*. 'This tug I'm in, it's probably the most efficient oil-rig auxiliary afloat. It has four engines of nearly three thousand horsepower. A bow engine to drive her astern. She rotates on herself and goes sideways. Given wings, she'd probably fly! But I love the *Mir-El-Lah*,' he added, stroking her woodwork.

He invited us aboard the *Austin Prince* for breakfast and on the way asked when I was sailing for Dubai.

'Any time now,' I answered.

'You'd better wait a day or two. It would be wiser.'

'Maybe. But I feel that by this evening we'll be in Dubai after a good sail,' I told him.

He shrugged. 'As you wish. But watch out. The entrance to the harbour is tricky and narrow.'

I suspected that, had he been with us instead of aboard that computerised tug, he would have encouraged me to sail right away.

In the chromium-plated, plastic-sheeted cafeteria we had an American breakfast of coffee, cornflakes and buns, and were joined by the skipper, a heavy-set man in his fifties. This was his first trip to the Old World, he told us in his deep Southern accent, and he hoped to God it was his last.

'Why, goddammit man,' he said, heaping his plate with cornflakes, 'there I was back home at Corpus Christi in Texas, my first day off in months watching television with my wife and gundog, when the darned telephone rings. And before I know it I'm on my way to some godforsaken place called Jazirath Farur on the other side of the world. I'm on loan to Continental Oil, hired by a French company, and that French company is chartered by Dubai Petroleum. When I was a kid my teacher told me all we Americans were free. I'm damned if that's freedom! You stay right aboard your dhow, man, with your pretty wife here. And don't charter yourself for no money to *anybody*! And that's the best piece of advice you'll ever get. Here, take this,' he added as he gave me a copy of the pilot charts he had been holding.

We said goodbye to the wise, weather-beaten Southerner and embraced Domenico, promising we would meet again soon in Dubai – *inshallah*.

Our anchors were firmly embedded in the sand and we were only able to weigh them by going forward on the engine. I am sure Domenico was watching us with a touch of pride – and envy – as we hoisted the sail, and then bore away before the wind, the lateen drawing well. The *Mir-El-Lah*, with practically no keel and without ballast, rode the sea like a skimming-dish; she was not difficult to steer, for she did not yaw or gybe when running before the wind.

So began one of the most perfect day's sailing I have ever had – and the fastest, for we were making almost twelve knots in complete comfort without shipping a drop of water.

On the way we sighted what at first appeared to be a whale lying on the surface until we drew nearer and saw it was the hull of the tanker that had capsized the night before. Alongside her was a tug flying the signals marking a wreck dangerous to shipping.

That day the *shamal* was kind to us, dying away as we approached the tankers and other vessels anchored outside the territorial waters of the Trucial States.

11. Dubai

Were we really just off Dubai and the entrance to Smugglers' Creek, or would we suddenly be confronted by the Statue of Liberty?

Mirella gasped: 'God, this is Manhattan!'

'You're seeing things. Here, read this,' I said, handing her the *Gulf Pilot* open at page 165.

Mirella read aloud: 'Dubai is situated a short distance inland, and from it a date grove extends for about two miles south-eastwards, terminating in a detached clump. Dera is a large suburb of mud huts, among which stand a number of well-built houses which have square towers with pillared tops. Two conspicuous minarets stand a short distance from the fort ...

She stopped reading. 'It goes on to say that in 1967 it was reported that new buildings had made it difficult to identify these landmarks. And that,' she added, 'must be the understatement of all time! Just look at that skyline!'

But, in spite of all the development, the dhows were still there. Three were converging on Smugglers' Creek in company with us; two were Pakistani dhows and one an old motorised *abubuz* without sails. I just managed to sneak in ahead of them after lowering and lashing the sail. The passage from Sirri had taken us half a day, a fast run by any standards.

Beyond the bustling creek several skyscrapers had appeared. Soon they would form an artificial canyon at the bottom of which the dhows would go on trading until they were replaced, one by one, by steel freighters.

Dubai is one of seven sheikhdoms: Abu Dhabi, Ajman, Umm-al-Qaiwan, Ras-al-Khaima, Sharja and Fujaira. A century ago this was the 'Pirate Coast', and mariners from Europe and Asia alike gave it a wide berth. In 1853, to protect the interests of the Honourable East India Company, a 'Treaty of Perpetual Peace' was signed with Great Britain, which I believe is still in force today. In ten years Dubai has changed more than any other place I know. India's thirst for gold smuggled from Dubai by dhows, and now the important oil discoveries, have brought so much wealth that skyscrapers and highways are replacing mud huts and minarets, camel tracks and a way of life that I am not sure was ready for sudden extinction.

At that moment, however, the world of the dhows was still very much alive and *Alhamdu l'illah* – 'Praise be to God' – there was enough past, enough people, mud huts, wind towers, old forts and minarets to make a physical contact with the old world I loved. In this particular case I felt completely out of tune with the view that progress is logical, necessary and natural. The human mind needs beauty as much as it needs food. In Dubai I was witnessing a change that would eventually transform many of the tough, sinewy desert people into greedy city dwellers and fat slobs. A Bedu with his camel in the desert is not the same man inside when he stands next to a Toyota in front of a skyscraper – and I will not allow anyone to tell me that I am just an incurable romantic.

In the canal there were so many dhows moored, four and six abreast, that we had to wait before we could find a berth while one of them, laden with melons from Karachi, discharged her cargo. Fortunately she was not long about it; there is a brisk market in Dubai for fruit and vegetables. As soon as she had moved out a host of willing Sinbads took our warps, clearly as fascinated by the mysterious flag the *Mir-El-Lah* was flying as by the white man at her wheel and the pretty European woman beside him. In no time we were moored amongst a great fleet of dhows of all shapes and sizes.

'This, Mirella, is the world of the dhow,' I said rather formally.

We planned to stay in Dubai for several weeks – I was tired and needed a rest. The film crew were impatient but I told them we must get our priorities right. First we had to overhaul the *Mir-El-Lah*'s shaft and make her thoroughly seaworthy.

Having made that clear, I went to find my old friend Kabul the carpenter and explained the trouble we had had with the shaft, owing to the engine seating being out of line. Then, once I had set him to work, I brought the Arab agent for Kubota aboard. (Kubota was the Japanese engine used in *Mir-El-Lah*.) He was wearing a spotless white *dish-dash* and after he had lowered himself into the engine-room I expected him to emerge black with grease; but five minutes later he appeared smiling and still spotless.

'*Taijib*,' he said. 'Everything is *taijib*. Kubota engines very good.'

'What about the pump?' I asked.

'*Taijib*.'

'And the starter?'

'*Taijib*,' came the inevitable answer.

I was not convinced, and it took me five years and fifteen thousand miles before I myself could decide whether everything was *taijib*. It was!

*

While Mirella was out with her cameras I went on a diving excursion to Ras-al-Khaima in a fishing dhow from Dubai. Friends had told me that an old German liner, the *Dara*, had been sunk some ten miles offshore in 1960, and three hundred passengers had gone down with her. Some of the skeletons aboard, they said, were still asleep in their cabins. And because their spirits haunted the wreck, fear kept the local divers from searching for the *Dara*'s gold in her cabins.

When we reached the wreck, marked by a buoy, the fishermen lowered their chicken-wire fish-traps, shaped like igloos and large enough to hold a horse standing inside.

Ignoring the usual warnings of sharks, I wore mask and fins to test the currents and the clarity of the water. Conditions were ideal. There was a flat calm and the water, which I had been told was usually murky, was crystal clear. But I was not to know how lucky I was for, although I later went to the trouble – and expense – of hiring Horace Dobbs, an underwater cameraman from London, to film the *Dara* for me, never again was I able to dive and see more than a few muddy feet away.

That morning after my reconnaissance, wearing a full diving kit, I went down again to experience the best dive of my long underwater career. The explosion that had caused the *Dara*'s end had split her into three pieces – bow, midships and stern. I found nothing sinister about the wreck that was fast becoming part of the seabed. I saw no skeletons, only fish in their thousands. Giant barracuda cruising in twos and threes, small barracuda in shoals. Red snappers up to twenty kilos, great rock cods peering at me from their caves, and the usual masses of small, colourful fish so thick that I had to scatter them to see my way through. On the seabed lay huge sting-rays, half buried in the fine white sand, put to sudden flight by the nose-poking guitar sharks. Keeping their distance I spotted some white-tip sharks and a twelve-to fifteen-foot tiger shark gliding in mid-water.

I also found the first of many lost fishing-traps. Currents and bad weather had fouled them up with the battered plates, derricks and frames of the *Dara*, rusting and thick with barnacles. One cage held prisoner a single great snapper that stared at me with sad eyes. I saw him as the Count of Monte Cristo of red snappers! I felt sorry for him and tried to free him but only succeeded in cutting my hand quite badly. My air was running out and I had to surface, trailing a green cloud of blood behind.

One of the first things we did in Dubai was to pay our respects to Sheikh Mohammed-al-Maktum, son of the supreme ruler, Rashid. In his official residence we were escorted into a large, sparsely furnished room on one side of which were a number of tanned British officers, the Sheikh's advisers, wearing desert uniforms topped by red-and-white *aghals*. Next to them sat visiting dignitaries from other emirates, local businessmen, falconers, and poor desert people whose simple ways and worn clothes stood out in sharp contrast to the expensive modern furniture and plate-glass windows. Bedouin bodyguards, wearing their traditional desert robes and clutching submachine-guns, stood at the four corners of the room.

Of all the people in the audience, the falconers were the most impressive. With hooded hawks perched on their wrists they stood like statues. Every once in a while a servant would bring out a glass of water on a silver tray for the birds to drink.

We waited as Sheikh Mohammed attended to his visitors. Everyone who was seeking a favour or a business deal had to state his case publicly. When it was our turn, Sheikh Mohammed listened with interest as I told him about our voyage from Khorramshahr and our desire to learn as much as we could about the world of the dhows.

To our disappointment, he explained how little their great sailing tradition meant to his people. Dhow-sailing was only romantic to foreigners, he said; in the Gulf dhows were of interest only because of the cargoes they were able to carry. Sailing was hard work, and sailors were just hard-working people; there was no romance attached to them. Now that there were easier ways to make a living in Dubai, the sailing tradition was becoming less important.

I was surprised at his remarks because the national emblem of Dubai was a dhow. When I reminded the Sheikh that the dhow was to be found on coins, flags, badges and stamps in most of the emirates and sheikhdoms of the Arab Peninsula, he said that the emblem would have to be changed.

'I shall replace it with a peregrine falcon,' he said. 'As you may have noticed, I am a great admirer of these birds. I hope that one day I will be able to take you to the desert to hunt *habaras* [lesser bustard].'

We did not have to wait long. The very next day a Range-Rover drove up to the *Mir-El-Lah* at seven in the morning and a dashing officer of the Desert Corps invited us to go on a hunting trip with Sheikh Mohammed. We were to come as we were – anything we needed during the trip the Sheikh would provide.

Half an hour later we were in his helicopter flying over the desert. To the north we could see mountains rising above the morning mist; all around us stretching to the horizon were golden sand dunes. We flew east, straight into the sun towards the Sea of Oman. To the west lay the Arabian Gulf. It was the nearest thing to sitting on a flying carpet beside an Arabian prince.

We landed near an oasis – a solitary well surrounded by tents and by falcons perched on short poles. We spent the afternoon resting and were offered no food or drink until the sun had set, for it was Ramadan, the Moslem month of fasting. In the evening, we sat on carpets sipping mint tea; young falcons were brought out for our inspection.

I had tried my hand at falconry many years before in Tunisia and was able to join in the discussions. The Sheikh was pleased to find I had a genuine interest in the sport, and before we retired for the night he suggested I accompany him to Pakistan, where the hunting was better.

When we awoke at six next morning the falconers and their hooded hawks were already seated in the Range-Rovers. Trackers had been out since daybreak in search of *habaras*, and when the first scout returned we set off across the sand at great speed. Half an hour later a *habara* took off from behind a bush; the falconer in our car removed the hood from the hawk's head and released him. The *habara* was flying slowly, close to the ground. Our falcon was still new to the game. It flew too high past the bustard without noticing it; when it did, it made a sharp turn, but too late. The *habara* rose high into the sky, the falcon after it. We watched the two birds climb until they were barely visible, then collide and fall together to the ground. Led by the Sheikh, we chased after them across the sand dunes. Finally we spotted our falcon sitting on its victim's body, pecking viciously at its brain and eyes.

Soon after our hunting expedition, Sheikh Mohammed introduced us to another local sport – camel racing. This was certainly the strangest sporting event I have ever witnessed. We were brought to the outskirts of the city, where a number of camels, jockeys, Land-Rovers and Mercedes had gathered. We watched this chaotic scene for well over an hour, then suddenly, without any warning, the camels took off, hotly pursued by the vehicles. Soon they had all disappeared, and we had no idea where they were going or when, if ever, they would come back. We never found out who won, and were not even sure that winning had anything to do with the 'race'.

By now we had become good friends with the Sheikh. When he was not able to entertain us himself, his personal pilot, a friendly Austrian named Gerhardt Trosch, took us on excursions in his helicopter. The most memorable of these trips was to Khor Fakkan on the Gulf of Oman. On our way we stopped off at several oases and rested in the shade of mud castles.

Overleaf Sheikh Rashid-al-Maktum, the ruler of Dubai, invited us to a camel race. I gambled £50 on this camel and lost

We flew over mountains, swooped down over deserted beaches and reefs and, towards evening, the pearl-oyster banks. We flew over a fiercely burning oil rig off the coast of Dubai. Red Adair, the famous American oil fire-fighter, blew it up a week later.

I had noticed that one of the Sheikh's helicopters – there were five at the airport – was pocked with bullet holes. Gerhardt explained to me that, although the seven Emirates were 'united', the ancient feuds between neighbouring sheikhdoms existed as much as ever. The enmity between Dubai and Sharja was notorious. Several months previously, when Sheikh Rashid – Mohammed's father – was building a road from Dubai to Khor Fakkan, the Sheikh of Sharja accused the Dubaians of taking water from a well he claimed was his. To make sure that they did not do so again he posted half a dozen guards round the well.

When Sheikh Mohammed heard of this, he and his English Deputy Air Commander flew to the well to see for themselves. Just as they were landing machine-guns opened fire. Hit repeatedly, the chopper crashed, and the two men had to run for their lives to the main road where a taxi gave them a lift back to Dubai. A few days later Sheikh Mohammed retaliated with an artillery barrage on the well, and so began another of the many rounds of hostilities. Peace was restored only when the old Sheikh of Sharja was shot dead in his palace by some of his own retinue.

Gerhardt explained that the hostility between the two sheikhdoms extended back to the turn of the century, when Sheikh Rashid's grandfather secured a trading contract from under the nose of the wavering Sheikh of Sharja, thus making Dubai the most important trading centre of the Arabian Gulf and the heart of the world of the dhows.

Dubai had also been the centre of the gold-smuggling trade. Almost two hundred tons of gold were flown in yearly from the gold capitals of Europe and transferred to India by dhows. As Dubai was a free import and export market for gold, this was quite legal; only when the dhows reached India did the business become illegal. The Indians' craze for gold-hoarding was depleting the national reserves so quickly that in 1947 its import was banned, after which the black market reached gigantic proportions. The dhows carrying gold were indistinguishable from the local fishing boats of India and Pakistan; they rarely visited ports and they held their assignations far off the coast.

We were having such a marvellous time in Dubai we put off our departure several times. Sheikh Mohammed prepared to leave on his annual falcon hunt in Pakistan; he invited us to go with him, but we had to refuse.

We went to see him off at the airport, which was packed with masses of pilgrims returning from Mecca, who were sprawled on the marble floors. The VIP lounge was crowded too. When we arrived Sheikh Mohammed brushed aside his officers and falconers to come and greet us.

We followed him into his private 707, where the sixty falconers were already seated, their hawks firmly clutching their padded wrists, the only passengers. A strange, incongruous sight, these fierce desert people wearing seat belts, their reverent '*Salaam aleikum*' echoing through the aircraft.

'Won't you reconsider my invitation?' Sheikh Mohammed asked. 'We shall only be gone a month.'

Sadly I shook my head, assuring him that I would regret it all my life. 'I have to sail for Africa before the weather breaks,' I said.

Overleaf Kumzar, in the Musandam peninsula, where a landslide ashore almost ended our lives. This is the heart of the world of the dhows

12. The Musandam Peninsula

We had been more than a month in Dubai, and all the Africa-bound dhows had already left. I was well aware that unless we sailed fairly soon I would have to cope with the south-eastern monsoon along the Somali coast.

The dhows had not left Dubai in convoy, for they travelled at different speeds and to different ports of call. Like migratory birds they had set off with the first big blow, and it was *Mir-El-Lah*'s turn to follow in their wake. I was more than ever conscious of my inexperience and responsibilities, for there were nine people on board now, including my two daughters, our 'Godfather' Roberto Gancia, and Bob Zagury from Paris, an old diving companion who had joined us in Dubai.

Our departure for the mysterious Musandam Peninsula was overshadowed for me by the loss of Ahmed and Shaiyad, who had both returned to Khorramshahr. They had been good and faithful companions through fair weather and foul, and I would miss them deeply.

I had replaced them – though at the time this seemed hardly the right term – with two Kenyans from Machakos, Madeka and Kimuyu, who had worked for me at Kilifi for over ten years. They were antelope hunters, and had never even seen the sea except from the deck of the SS *Cementia*, coming from Mombasa to Dubai. They could not swim, and, quite cleverly, each had taken the precaution of bringing a life-jacket, their only baggage.

I had hired two illegal Indian immigrants to teach them the rudiments of seamanship. They claimed to be from Madras and told me their ancestors had owned dhows even before the days of the Prophet Mohammed and that they themselves had sailed in dhows since they were born. But they displayed little expertise that morning when we left Dubai. At first I thought maybe they were shy; they smiled a lot, nodding their heads at everything I said. But when we met the open sea and the *Mir-El-Lah* began to roll gently their faces turned a sickly shade of green. When I discovered they could not even tell the wheel from the sail I lost my temper. They quickly confessed that they were Indian army deserters from Delhi and had never been to sea before except as passengers.

Well, there I was with a crew of four, the most experienced of them my two antelope hunters from the hills of Machakos. I felt like casting my deserters adrift in the dinghy with some bread and water. But the dinghy was too valuable, so the next day I deposited them on the pier of Ras-al-Khaima. As I paid them one week's wages for charity's sake (and restrained myself from kicking their backsides) I wondered how I was ever going to make it to Africa. How was I to get any sleep? If Allah wanted me to sail the *Mir-El-Lah* to Mombasa it was up to Him to solve my problems! After all, I reflected, the crews of most of the dhows I had seen in Dubai were ex-slaves from the East African coast; to a certain extent I was following in the old traditions.

After leaving the two deserters at Ras-al-Khaima, I set a course well clear of the land and the many sandbanks and wrecks; some thirty miles out to sea, sailing parallel with the coast. I missed Ahmed, and when darkness fell I longed to have him by my side.

I was for ever turning to the *Pilot*, but its ominous warnings did little to relieve my anxiety. It told of unpredictable winds, adverse currents up to four knots, sharp pinnacles of rocks, unfriendly cave-dwellers and heavy rains ...

But how much could I rely on this information? Had Essoville and Shelltown replaced the fishermen's huts in Khasab Bay and Kumzar? The fact that the *Pilot* stated there was no oil in such areas did not exclude efforts to prospect for it!

That night a bad navigational error sent me miles off course. I had measured my course on two different charts, assuming wrongly that they had the same scale. At four in the morning I decided to head due east and, after sighting land, to search for an anchorage in one of the many fjords that break up the Musandam Peninsula like the fingers of an outstretched hand.

At sunrise we neared black mountains towering above a steel-grey sea with blue peaks rising higher and higher in the distance. The first rays of the sun flashed between them like searchlights. We recognised Khawr Khasab, the long, deep fjord leading to the capital of the Musandam. The sea was a mirror reflecting the mountains, the clouds and dazzling sunlight: the fjords

of Norway and the Grand Canyon of Arizona in one single vision. There was the powerful silence of the great cathedrals. Overhead, fishing eagles floated in the thermals.

Mirella and I sat on the bow, spellbound by the majestic beauty of this enchanted land we were discovering. From time to time I gave directions to Madeka at the wheel for, according to the charts, the water shallowed quickly at the fjord so that we had to drop anchor some distance offshore beneath the old, square sand-coloured fort of Khasab. On its ramparts ancient muzzle-loading cannons faced seawards. To herald our arrival one of them went off with a resounding bang and a cloud of black smoke, yet no chained cannon-balls whizzed past. We found out later it was their custom to salute arriving vessels with a blank shot.

We lowered the dinghy and waded ashore leaving Kimuyu beneath the fort where two small *sambuks* were beached, awaiting the tide to refloat them. Two of the governor's bodyguards met us at the gates. Tall, dignified, bearded men, they were armed with rifles and *khanjars* – long, curved knives – in elaborate scabbards of leather, silver and gold, prized Omani possessions.

I presented my letters of introduction to the Wali (governor) of Musandam. Impressed by these documents, typed in Arabic, the guards examined them from all angles, folding and unfolding them; they finally returned them to me crumpled and greasy before escorting us on to the ramparts of the fort, from where we could look down on the *Mir-El-Lah* lying at anchor and Kimuyu fishing from the dinghy, holding the line between his toes.

While we waited, a runner was despatched to the Wali to inform him that friendly infidels had landed with letters to the Sultan. A Toyota land cruiser arrived in a cloud of dust, its engine roaring, and a handsome, clean-shaven young man came running up the steps to greet us in fluent English.

'Welcome, welcome to Khasab! I am the Wali; please come to my home. It is not far,' he invited us, spreading his arms wide.

Khasab must be the smallest capital in the world. It consists of half a dozen military barracks and an equal number of mud huts, while the 'palace' is little more than a prefabricated hut, totally out of keeping with its surroundings, and furnished with plastic armchairs and nylon carpets. But the Wali was a charming host. He gave us sickly sweet *halva* that carried in it the scent of languorous harems, with very black, bitter coffee which was served by a shy little girl who kept her eyes on the floor.

As we talked of our plans to make a film about dhows and the dhow

Opposite On the pier of Ras-al-Khaima, an old woman stared at me, a white *nakhoda*
Overleaf Indian dhows are better built than Arab ones, but much of the romance of dhow-building has gone

people, the Wali listened, slightly amused and surprised at our interest in things he took so much for granted.

'Yes, you are right. The world is changing so very fast,' he finally agreed, a little sadly. 'Only the Musandam remains the same. That is because they have discovered no oil. No oil, no money – nothing. Strategically, yes: we control the Strait of Hormuz with our guns! Tankers go by every five minutes, but none of them stops here. Oman has been opened to the world for only five years and maybe things will begin to change.'

Before we left his house he presented us with the flag of the Omani Sultanate and suggested we flew it at all times, for strange things could happen in his country, he warned, and from now on we should be careful.

'Never let the dhows surround you – never at night,' he told us, not explaining why, but apologising for not being able to offer more protection.

'Be kind enough to ask my friend Sheikh Omer in Muscat to send me word of your arrival. We have very little means of communication between here and Muscat. And, yes, you must visit Kumzar where the fishing is very good.'

The Wali accompanied us back to the beach and we spent our first night in the Musandam under the protection of six cannons left by the Portuguese centuries ago.

The next day at dawn we followed the Shamm Peninsula along the coast to Khawr Jhubb Ali, dropping anchor at the end of yet another four-mile-long fjord. The water was so clear we could see our anchors gripping the sand twenty feet below. Small, brilliantly coloured fish nibbled at them, while the surface reflected all the pink and mauve, violet and aquamarine shadows of the surrounding mountains.

Mirella went wild with her camera; such beauty was almost too much to absorb. I wanted to stay for weeks and weeks, concentrating each day on a different mountain, a different stretch of water.

I shall always remember that first day at Khawr Jhubb Ali. Roberto, far from the reach of telephones and telexes, slept. Kimuyu dozed, waking only when a fish snapped at the line between his toes. Only Madeka remained active, polishing the engine with loving care, ceaselessly singing his theme song, 'This land is not my home ... I'm just a-passing through ...' He liked to say of himself that he was the son of nobody. When he was ten his father, a driver on our farm in Kenya, ran away leaving his mother, brothers and sisters to fend for themselves.

Towards sunset the local fishing boats came home: long and slender with elaborately carved bows and decorated with patterns of white cowrie shells

Opposite We were going to meet the Wali of Khasab when a woman looked our way
Previous page The *serang* (boatswain) of the boom *El Mansur* in Muscat harbour

set in the woodwork. The Portuguese influence was also visible in their long thin oars with square paddles.

They hauled their boats up the greased logs on the beach. A purple mist descended on the village as the sun went down, the water turned from red to black, and the sky filled with stars that seemed to grow larger and larger as the night wore on.

Soon after first light, without waking the others, Bob and I set out for the mouth of the fjord in the dinghy with our diving gear. We made our first dive as the sun rose, descending into the fantastic world of sub-tropical coral formations.

I had hardly time to look around before I saw an old rusty anchor chain draped over a rocky ledge. Following it down, I found the huge anchor itself, in good condition complete with its ring. It must have been six feet in height, just right for the *Mir-El-Lah*. We raised it with the hoisting parachute filled with air from our aqualungs.

When we surfaced Bob told me he had seen some old timbers half buried in the sand. We secured the anchor to the dinghy and dived again. This time, we found the wreck of an old dhow: judging by the length of her keel she must have been sixty or seventy feet overall. Her remains were so encrusted with oysters and coral that we reckoned she must have gone down at least half a century ago.

With difficulty I managed to cut off a chip from one of the timbers with my knife. It was teak of the finest quality. Near it we found fragments of pottery, plates and vases. So excited were we with our wreck that Bob and I spent two days diving and filming it. While we were sawing the keel into two pieces, several small sharks came to inspect us; one of them attempted to snatch a fish from Bob's spear. I shot at him and missed – the shark glided between my legs and disappeared into the blue waters beyond.

With the combined efforts of the winch of the *Mir-El-Lah*, the parachute and two forty-four-gallon drums filled with air, we hoisted the two great beams aboard, only to find they took up most of the deck.

We sailed past the five fingers that form the bays of Fordna, Qalta, Ran and Kumzar, and returned to explore the bay of Kumzar and its village, accompanied by a school of playful porpoises, diving under our bows and leaping into the air in showers of sparkling spray. From the sea Kumzar seems a place from the Old Testament. On the beach lay a line of slim, elegant fishing boats, behind them the mud huts flanked by houses that appeared to be carved out of the mountainside. We dropped our anchors

Previous page Muscat, the capital of Oman. Was Sinbad born here?

twenty yards from the beach and went ashore.

As soon as they saw us, the villagers came running to the water's edge. The women hid behind the fishing boats, peeping at us; the men stood proudly erect with children clinging to their white *dish-dashes*. These, we believed, were the Shihuh, the people who had come to the Arab Peninsula long before the Arabs, and who were reputed to be the descendants of Ham. Such was their isolation that they had retained their way of life over the centuries. Indeed, little was known of their language or culture, beyond the fact that they had an 'inordinate fondness for knives'.

In Dubai we were told the only way to ensure a friendly reception from the Shihuh was to dispense kitchen knives, toys and medicaments. After showing our credentials to the local chieftain, we began by making the children happy with plastic toys and sweets, and dealt out aspirins, cod liver oil pills, mild laxatives and cough syrup from the medicine chest to the men and women. I wondered what they did when they needed a doctor. Later I learned that a hospital dhow is periodically sent from Muscat to visit and help these forgotten people.

Several young Shihuhis offered to lead us towards the hills. The view from the first of the fortified terraces was so magnificent that I decided to organise a trek to the top, to sleep that night in the mountains and return the next day. Aboard the *Mir-El-Lah*, we prepared for the expedition. With blankets, food and water, our cameras, binoculars and film we set out, dressed in tennis shoes, shorts, hats and sunglasses.

Our trek started up a narrow gully covered in loose slippery stones; a swarm of noisy children followed us and brought up the rear. When we reached the first terrace we had to climb up what looked like a spiral staircase cut into the soft rock which led along the side of the steep mountain. Since our guides were more interested in Mirella and her incessant photography than they were in leading us, I soon found myself a long way ahead of everyone. But as there was clearly only one way to go and I was feeling in good form, I saw no reason why I should not continue climbing and wait for the others when I reached the summit.

There were several caves cut into the mountain, their entrances blocked with neat piles of loose rocks. I wondered whether they were ancient graves and decided to explore them inside. It was pitch dark and smelt dank. I struck a match and just before it burned out I saw skulls and bones. Fearing that the Shihuh might resent my intrusion I left the caves and found myself in a large quarry. Above me rose a steep ledge of six hundred feet of loose rock. As I staggered on over the rough ground, I heard a rustling sound above me and a stone crashed past. Then, as the rocks under my feet began to move I made a dash for a stony pinnacle to my right and clung to it. The rustle quickly became a roar as great chunks of rock bounced by, gathering speed as they thundered past like a river in spate and disappeared over the precipice. God, I thought, I must have started an avalanche that will crush everyone below! Mirella and all those children buried beneath the great piles of rock . . .

Then I heard voices: just voices, not screams of pain. I heard Mirella calling my name. She was safe! They were safe! But I dared not move for fear of starting another landslide. I clung to my rock pinnacle, calling out and waiting for one of the Shihuh to reach me. He led me back to the path, from where I looked down on the other guides making their way towards me followed by Mirella in her flowered *kikoi*.

Mirella and I grabbed each other.

'My God, I thought you were dead!' we said simultaneously.

The landslide had missed Mirella by a dozen yards. At the bottom of the gully, the children were dancing up and down, laughing and pointing to the small hill of stones and rocks still smoking in a cloud of dust.

'So much for our trek and our night out on the mountain. Let's go back to the sea!' I said, as we made our way down to the beach, led by the villagers.

As if to make up for my narrow escape from death, the fishermen invited me to go out with them the next morning. We left Kumzar at dawn and sailed down the coast to an inlet with a beach of fine sand. From two of the longboats we spread a great net in a wide semi-circle. Weighted by stones with floaters at either end and long manilla ropes attached to its four corners, fully extended it stretched the width of the inlet; the ropes were led to the beach where fifteen men waited to handle them. Two others climbed the cliffs at either side of the cove, as lookouts.

I had already seen this method of fishing in Sardinia. I knew the technique well, having once observed it from underwater, allowing myself to be caught and dragged ashore with the fish.

There followed a long wait under the burning heat of the sun. We scanned the sea; a pair of eagles, circling slowly on the down-currents from the surrounding hills, watched with us.

Suddenly a loud shout repeated by echoes came from one of the men on the cliffs, as the other waved his arms. Jumping to their feet, the men began to haul, lying back on their manilla ropes until their heads were almost touching the sand, as if competing in a tug-of-war. As they closed ranks, coming shoulder to shoulder, hauling with all their strength, the net closed with them. Its bulging belly was seething with fish flashing silver. Kingfish – hundreds of them. I have never seen so many.

Up to their knees in the water, the men poured the fish into the longboats. The net was cast four times and several hundred kingfish were brought in that afternoon. When their labours were over, the men all gathered on the beach facing Mecca and bent down on the pebbly surface to say their evening prayer. When they had finished, I noticed that one of the oldest of them was being helped towards me. He was blind, but he had heard my outboard engine and begged me to take him with me back to Kumzar, for he loved the feeling of speed.

As soon as we were under way, he clapped his hands like an excited child. '*Alhamdu l'illah*,' he said, grinning with delight. When I left him outside his mud hut he kissed my hands; then, lifting his hands to the sky, he held a long conversation with God.

That night as we sat on the *Mir-El-Lah*'s deck, some unknown Sinbads passed us singing a beautiful song that echoed faintly in the great stone surroundings that stretched around us. It sounded like a Moorish song, with a touch of Spain and Sicily, far more melodious than the traditional wailing we had heard everywhere in the Gulf. A song without boundaries. The song of the dhows.

13. The Indian Ocean

A school of porpoises welcomed us into the Indian Ocean, and as we watched the youngsters pirouetting in the clear water I caught a glimpse of a magnificent black marlin that sailed right past our bows. We couldn't have had a more perfect greeting!

We had at last left the Arabian Gulf, entering the Ocean via the Fakk-al-Asad and the Ras-al-Bab. The Strait of Fakk-al-Asad is only three cables wide and, because of the strong currents and fickle winds from the mountains, navigation is a tricky business. As usual the *Pilot* was full of ominous warnings, this time against the multitude of rocky and largely invisible islets; it suggested that even shallow-draught vessels should keep as close to mid-channel as possible.

After a full day's sailing under perfect conditions we anchored for the night in Shabus Bay, yet another fjord of great beauty, where we sighted a village almost as big as Kumzar. The *Gulf Pilot* told us it was called Balad Shabus; no more, no less.

We dropped anchor several times in the evening but it dragged so badly we had to sail on for about a mile before we found a good holding-ground. I did not like to anchor too far from the village but my friends and crew were tired and did not fancy spending the night drifting back and forth.

At about five in the morning I was awakened by Madeka, who told me that another dhow had dropped anchor close to us, too close for his liking. '*Hatari*,' he said – danger.

I went on deck armed with my .22 pistol and twelve-bore shotgun, remembering the Wali of Khasab's warning about never allowing strange dhows to creep up on us. With my artillery beside me, I lay down in the bows and dozed until daylight. When the sun rose, the men on the dhow's decks looked harmless enough, and what interest they showed in us was directed towards our women when they appeared for breakfast.

Wishing to be friendly, I waved to them and invited them to come aboard. They immediately hauled on their anchor and as they approached threw us a warp so that we could pull them alongside. Twenty-five scraggy-looking men quickly swarmed over our deck, picking up and touching everything that was not either nailed or glued to the deck. When one of them showed particular interest in the T-shirt Mirella was wearing and started fingering it, I decided the time had come to make a move. Brandishing my weapons, I jumped on to the engine-room hatch and shouted at them to get off my dhow. Unfortunately they could not understand me so, ordering Madeka to start the engine, I fired both barrels of the twelve-bore well over their heads, while Bob harangued them, using every Arabic word in his limited vocabulary. Shrugging their shoulders, the 'pirates' departed quickly, convinced, I am sure, that we were lunatics, judging by the speed with which they hoisted sail and headed out to sea!

Mirella was disappointed when Bob vetoed any suggestion of landing to visit the village. We were too cut off from civilisation, and should the inhabitants here prove unfriendly we would have been at their mercy.

Later in the day, on our way to Ras Lima, a dhow flying the ensign of the Omani Navy overtook us. She was equipped with radar, powered by twin engines, and had a big Vickers gun mounted amidships – her gunners wore blue overalls and the crew were dressed in *dish-dashes* and red-checked Omani turbans. She was travelling at about twelve knots; we exchanged salutes as she passed.

All we knew of Ras Lima was that according to the *Pilot* it was 'a fishing village three and a half cables away from the Island of Lima and, like that island, mountainous. When HMS *Cyclamen* and HMS *Fowey* had visited it in 1922 and 1934 respectively, its inhabitants had proved friendly.'

However, this somewhat ludicrous description left us unprepared for the golden beaches, red mountains, coral reefs, virgin beds of pearl oysters and jumping schools of *bonito*.

The next morning I had one of the best dives of my life; as impressive as that on the wreck of the *Dara*, and yet very different. Here there were no sad remains of a lost ship, no thoughts of skeletons or their ghosts. I found myself swimming in a flowering rock garden amongst masses of coloured fish. On the north side of the islet I discovered coral reefs and rocks festooned with oysters, with very large and well-rounded shells.

I brought up over two hundred of them, and Madeka and Kimuyu spent the whole afternoon prising them open looking for pearls. But we found none. Our disappointment was soon forgotten as we settled down on deck under the full moon to eat a dozen crayfish Bob had speared.

The following day my daughter Marina and I went ashore on a beach carpeted with millions of sardines laid out by fishermen to dry in the sun. Battalions of gulls swooped from above, gorging themselves. Their shrieks echoed round the hills as they battled with each new flock of raiders over their territory.

From the beach, we climbed a very steep sandy hill and looked down on the *Mir-El-Lah* riding at anchor some four hundred feet below. With a yell of unsuppressed joy my daughter Marina hurled herself into the sand and I followed suit. Together, we tobogganed down the slope on our backsides, gathering speed faster and faster until we reached the bottom. Our twin tracks on the hillside looked like those left by some prehistoric monster.

The moment was approaching when our party would break up and I would be alone with Madeka and Kimuyu. Roberto had gone to the village of Lima to arrange for transport to pick up the others as soon as we landed at Khor Fakkan. Their plane was leaving from Dubai in two days' time.

I was sad to see the row of suitcases on the deck, sadder still when I watched through binoculars the Land Rover drive away from the shore at Khor Fakkan. Then I noticed a man walking on the beach, and as he approached I saw to my utter amazement that it was my old friend 'San' Lorenzo Berni from London. He waved and shouted something I could not hear. What, in the name of Allah, was he doing in Khor Fakkan?

Suddenly I remembered our conversation on my last night in London when we had dined together in his restaurant and I had drunk more than my share of two bottles of Vernaccia. We had talked of dhows and I had invited him to come sailing with me in the *Mir-El-Lah*. As we rambled on late into the night I had drawn a map of the Musandam Peninsula on a paper napkin and scribbled the name Khor Fakkan. 'Meet me there on January 7th,' I had said, never really believing I would keep the appointment or that he would take it seriously. It was now January 7th; Lorenzo was there and I was there too. It must have been written in the stars.

Next morning at dawn we left for Muscat. Like me, San Lorenzo was looking forward to seeing that fabled city which had been virtually a forbidden place since Don Duarte de Menenez, Viceroy and Governor of India, had left it in 1558.

As usual, the *Pilot* was enigmatic. 'The coastline is rocky and precipitous, there are towers and castles crowning some of the overlooking peaks. The town is situated at the head of the Khawr Muscat, but it does not show up well under the dark hills...'

I laid my course directly towards the islands of Saba, then, having turned the wheel over to Kimuyu, I lay down on a mattress beside him to sleep, as I always did when one of my men was steering. I was rudely awakened by Madeka kicking me in the backside and shouting '*Hatari! Hatari sana!*' ('Danger! Great danger!')

Jumping to the wheel, I peered into the night and suddenly found myself staring at a huge black rock, less than a hundred feet ahead. It was Jazirath Kharabah, a rock clearly marked on the chart that I had reckoned on sighting at dawn. I realised then that a favourable current had carried the *Mir-El-Lah* along so fast during the night that we had reached this dangerous rock hours ahead of schedule.

I grabbed the wheel and veered hard to starboard. I handed it back to Madeka and raced forward to make certain we were well clear of the rock which was looming dangerously close. As I did so I gashed my foot on the bilge-pump filter that some idiot (probably myself) had left lying about. By morning my foot was inflamed and double its normal size and I had all the symptoms of blood poisoning. Fortunately, San Lorenzo carried an impressive supply of antibiotics and fed me a large dose of pencillin for breakfast.

We passed the island of Fahl, the Omani oil terminal, and proceeded into Matrah harbour, the brand-new seaport of Muscat. The first thing we saw was a fleet of bright yellow bulldozers demolishing the last remains of legendary Muscat, known to the Arabs as a city of poets and lovers. My heart sank with our two anchors to the bottom of the harbour. We had arrived too late.

Up till July 1970, the gates of the old city of Muscat were closed every evening three hours after sunset, when a cannon was fired three times as a warning. After that, no one was allowed to walk in its streets unless carrying a hurricane lantern, and those caught without one were jailed for the night.

An official publication handed out to us when we went ashore stated blandly that much of the old Muscat had been razed to the ground to make way for the essential buildings of a progressive age, and the grandest of these was to be the new palace of His Majesty the Sultan. This, I saw, was nearing completion and it seemed to me almost a replica of the Monte Carlo Casino!

Ironically, in the *Gulf Pilot* I read that 'Row upon row of rugged mountains stretch into the distance and, nestling in a small bay where the mountains meet the sea, stands the walled city of Muscat.'

That walled city was now a scattered mass of rubble and, as I looked at the desolation, I tried to imagine how Muscat must have been centuries before when Marco Polo had remarked that its harbour was packed with dhows and the eastern sea-lanes were dangerously congested. At least, thank God, there were still a good many dhows in the harbour. At some distance from where we were anchored lay the largest and most beautiful dhow I had ever seen. I took the dinghy and rowed over to her.

She was a *baghla* from Sur with two towering masts, her high transom magnificently carved and decorated, as were the five square ports of her after-cabin. When I climbed on to her sweeping deck I felt I was aboard a ghost ship: there was not a soul on board – not a sign of life below deck, no cargo, no engine, no crew's belongings, nothing. I spent an hour carefully looking over this jewel of the sea that must have been at least a hundred years old. Her rigging was perfect and her sails neatly furled, and everywhere lovely, intricately carved woodwork. I took my knife and cut a chip from her bulwarks and found to my astonishment that beneath the patina of age the wood was like new. It was not until I visited the harbourmaster's office that I solved the mystery of the phantom ship. The harbourmaster, an Englishman, told me she had been bought for a mere five thousand pounds by Sultan Qabus, who planned to find a suitable resting-place where, like Nelson's *Victory*, she could be preserved for posterity.

Later in the day, San Lorenzo and I explored the bazaar of Muscat. Any dreams we had of finding carpets, silver and spices from the East were quickly shattered. At stall after stall, all we saw were plastic toys from Japan, shoddy suits from Taiwan, cheap cotton goods from India and Pakistan, and trashy jewellery from Hong Kong.

Disillusioned, we turned our backs on the bearded, wary-eyed merchants and elbowed our way through the crowded streets, as we searched for the Sheikh whom the Wali of Musandam had said we must meet. We found him in his office. A charming and dignified Zanzibari, Sheikh Omer Ameir was head of Information and Broadcasting. He told us how he had fled from his native clove island in the Indian Ocean when the 'original inhabitants' had taken over, and he was now permanently settled in Oman.

The Sheikh told us something of the country's history. He began with the arrival of the Portuguese in the fifteenth century. Their excuse, like that of the British, Dutch and French who followed later, was to open up a new trade route to India, but in fact they were more interested in conquest. In

1507 when Alfonso de Albuquerque arrived off Ras-al-Hadd, his first act was to set fire to the fleet of fishing dhows which had come from the cities of Hormuz and Bandar Abbas in Iran.

Such behaviour led to a series of skirmishes that culminated in the declaration of a holy war against the invaders. The Omani Sultans pursued their enemies along the eastern coast of Africa and the western coast of India, capturing so many ships – including some of the Honourable East India Company – that their navy soon became the most powerful in the Indian Ocean.

It was not until the beginning of the nineteenth century that peace was made with the Sultans and the British moved in to consolidate their position in Oman. By keeping faith with them Sultan Sayyid Said was able to travel widely and expand his Sultanate by conquering Dhofar. 'The King of Dhows,' our friend the Sheikh called him, for he spent most of his life sailing from one African possession to another in his dhow until, in his old age, he settled in Zanzibar. The British agreed to maintain order in Oman only if the Sultan would abolish the highly profitable slave trade between his African territories and Arabia. Sayyid Said consented, to the ruination of the Omani economy. By the time he died in 1856 his splendid fleet of dhows had dwindled to only a few vessels.

Sheikh Omer Ameir told us all this and much more that morning in his office while we drank little cups of strong, bitter coffee. Then he invited us to visit the interior of Oman. 'In the villages life is still the same, untouched by the modern age,' he told us, as if reading our thoughts about the demolition of his old walled city.

'When you leave our coasts, sail straight for Africa,' he warned. 'Stay out at sea. Above all, stay away from South Yemen.'

14. The Coast of Arabia

It was now almost the end of January and I was living in dread of having to battle against the monsoon before I reached Lamu. I set sail for Sur, home of the most famous of all dhow builders. Once under way, I turned to the dog-eared pages of the *Pilot*. Sur, it assured me, would be 'hard to find' although only half a day's sail from Muscat.

On the way we caught a large *bonito* and San Lorenzo taught Kimuyu how to cut it in thin, almost transparent slices, which he covered with olive oil and lemon juice and left for two hours to cook in the sun.

According to the *Pilot*, Sur consisted of a group of settlements at the mouth of the Wadi Falaij river. I sighted a dhow lying a mile off the low sandy coast and hailed her crew to ask for directions. They pointed landwards, but when I scanned the coast I could see no sign of the river nor any landmark that might help find it.

Eventually it dawned on me that the dhow was waiting for high water, and sure enough, just as Kimuyu had produced our five o'clock tea, the dhow's sleeping crew came alive and started hauling in her anchors. Following suit, we got under way, trailing her for a mile up the coast to a small inlet up which we were swept inland by a strong current until we were abreast of a solitary house. Like our leader, we dropped two anchors in the stream to hold us against the currents, one ahead and one astern.

Once ashore we asked for Sur. The men crouching around the house pointed to a marshy plain, deserted except for a few camels and a donkey. In the distance I could see another solitary house. I simply could not believe that all the magnificent Suri dhow builders were hidden behind it. I trudged over to it, only to find more marshes, more camels and more donkeys.

I stopped everyone I met and showed them photographs of dhows, *sambuks*, *booms*, *baghlas* and *abubuzis*. I produced Villiers' *Sons of Sinbad*. I was greeted with nods, suggestions in Arabic, smiles. I was offered dates and camel's milk. One Arab even took my photograph, but nobody could tell me anything about dhow building in the area.

Sadly I decided to leave the next day at dawn. But it was not to be: the current of the muddy river had caused one of our anchors to foul that of the nearby dhow. Only after several hours were we able to disentangle it and head out into the Indian Ocean, where a fresh fair wind revived our spirits.

As I studied the chart I realised that there was no land between us and the South Pole. Had I held my present course I could have sailed all the way to Antarctica without ever sighting land. Instead I turned right towards Ras-al-Hadd.

This is a small village near a huge fort – beautiful and deserted. After reading the last page of my old *Pilot*, which described some fearsome currents, San Lorenzo and I agreed to make for Masirah Island. I closed the *Gulf Pilot* and felt as if I were burying a dear friend when I put it away in a drawer. I opened my new companion, the *Red Sea and Gulf of Aden Pilot*, 'comprising the Red Sea, the Gulf of Aden, the Suez Canal, the Gulf of Suez and Aqaba, the south-east coast of Arabia from Ras Baghashwa to Ras-al-Hadd, the coast of Africa from Ras Asir to Ras Hafun, Soccotra and its adjacent islands'.

The first entry in this book dealt with the Masirah channel we were about to enter. It was scarcely reassuring with its warnings of many inlets and rocks, and the suggestion that only small vessels with local knowledge should attempt the passage. This was followed by an ominous list of wrecks: the SS *Electra*, whose two masts and funnel were still visible in 1962, the SS *World Jury*, well known as a radar target, and the *Baron Inverdale*, whose crew had been murdered by the people of Masirah in 1904.

The entry dealing with Masirah itself offered little comfort. It described it as 'barren and sterile and teeming with lizards, snakes and scorpions', its beaches popular only with the turtles that came ashore in their thousands to lay eggs. Even the sea, it reported, was alive with sharks and barracuda.

Such an uninviting prospect was not improved when a dense haze, which rapidly thickened to fog, descended on us, so that from the *Mir-El-Lah's* wheel I could barely see her bows, let alone the rocks, reefs and wrecks. Instead of searching for an 'unspoiled' harbour, we opted for the RAF base at the northern end of the island.

With the engine dead slow, we felt our way through the low-hanging fog.

Above it we could hear the roar of aircraft. Then, as suddenly as it had descended, the fog lifted and we saw a barren hill, a high metal fence, and a beach not more than a hundred yards ahead. Just as we dropped anchor some twenty jet fighters swooped down from the clouds, barely missing our mast and clearing the fence by a few feet before climbing vertically back into the clouds again.

In the fog we had sighted what we took to be a wreck, but as it gave way reluctantly to the sun and the light breeze we saw that our wreck was a Royal Navy supply ship. We rowed over to her in the dinghy and were told by her crew that Masirah was only some two miles away. Landing on the beach, we found a lone sentry-box; its occupant was a pink-faced young Scot wearing over-long shorts, bush shirt and beret, who greeted us with the traditional, 'Who goes there?', examined our documents, apologised politely for challenging us, and telephoned the base.

After Kharg, it was a relief to be treated so courteously and we were astonished when, in answer to the sentry's call, a jeep arrived with three RAF military police accompanied by a civilian. They politely suggested we should anchor for the night off the village where the Governor of Masirah, the Wali, lived. They pointed out their barracks, the stores, the post office and told us their facilities were at our disposal.

The following day, surrounded by bodyguards, we called on the Wali at his small, modern house. It reminded me of the home of a Spanish peasant where I had once slept near Toledo. Its décor was as simple and unpretentious as its owner – white walls, plain furniture, bowls of fruit and boiled rice on the table and a jug of milk. He was a happy, friendly man who lived alone in his house. He introduced us to his guests: two young Bedus who went to school in England, and a tall New Zealander who roamed the desert in search of water wells.

He looked like Lawrence of Arabia in his Arab clothing. When I asked him why he liked the desert he answered, as Lawrence had done to the same question: 'Because it is clean.'

The Wali, accompanied by his bodyguards, took us on a tour of the town in his Land-Rover. We stopped at the memorial to the forty-seven victims of the *Baron Inverdale* massacre: a plain iron cross over a pile of rocks, bearing the strange inscription 'To the survivors who did not survive'.

The Wali expressed great interest in the *Mir-El-Lah*. We invited him and his entourage on board. Kimuyu laid out carpets and cushions on the deck and served tea on a large silver tray. The supreme ruler of Masirah sat back, enjoying the lovely view, while we discussed the land, the desert, the sea, the turtles, and the world. The sun set. No one moved. The magic hour, the hour when the sky begins to darken and the first breeze of the evening cools the air, came and went. Finally, as darkness fell, we took our guests ashore. As we bade them farewell, I made the mistake of admiring one of the bodyguard's magnificent *khanjar*. Immediately, he took it from his belt and presented it to me. Embarrassed, I hesitated until, at risk of offending him, I accepted it. Now it is one of my most treasured possessions.

In the dark, San Lorenzo and I were guided back to the *Mir-El-Lah* by the sound of Kimuyu's laughter. On board we found him, still roaring with laughter, in the galley. He had caught a four-pound sucker fish. The back of this creature looks like the rubber sole of a sneaker, complete with all the symmetrical zig-zags. Its suction glands were so powerful that when we put it on Kimuyu's stove it took the three of us to wrench it free.

I approached the next stage of our voyage to Salalah, some four hundred miles away, with some apprehension, for both the Wali and the RAF had warned me to keep well out to sea. The country was wild, they said, and inhabited by unfriendly, trigger-happy nomads whose code of honour towards strangers could be summed up as 'he who shoots first laughs last'.

'We don't want any more monuments to dead mariners,' the Station Commander remarked laconically as I thanked him for his kindness.

We sailed along until we reached the Kuria Muria Islands. These islands were to me what trees are to birds: a tempting place to land. They had to be approached with caution, for although they were British possessions only Hallania was known to be 'civilized'. The other islands, Suda, Garzanth and Hazikia, had between them at the last count a population of only fifty-five, all described as 'unfriendly'. The only other living creatures on the islands were blue-faced boobies.

To port was the Rub al Khali – the Empty Quarter – thousands upon thousands of shifting sand dunes. We knew it was there although we could not see it: the loneliness of the vast desert seemed to haunt us even at sea. Never before had I felt so lonely, so far away. When I sighted the four-peaked rock of Qibliya, the first of the islets, there were no signs of life. I fired two shots into the air. The sky filled with clouds of boobies which took off in fluffy flashes of silver light.

We sailed on round the islands, whose rock formations rose out of the sea like modern sculptures. We trawled our fishing lines and hauled in a huge kingfish. From the Kuria Muria Islands we headed towards the mainland, to Ras Marabat at the foot of the Jabal Samban mountain range that rises to

Overleaf Madeka (*right*) and Kimuyu. I owe them, my two African soul brothers, some of the best moments of my life. This book is for them both. Without them there would be no story or perhaps an unpleasant one of hardship, bad food and survival

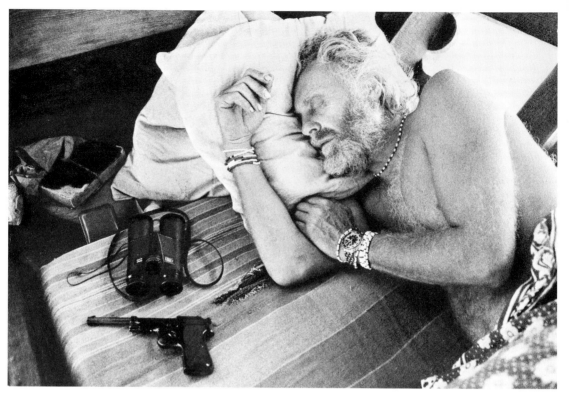

We often moored in places where I felt better sleeping with my artillery beside me

four thousand feet. These mountains were some distance inland, and
between them and the sea lay an invisible coastal plain. I did not realise I was
sailing dangerously close to the shore. But on that silvery night it was not
written in the stars that we should perish.

I was dozing when Kimuyu shook me violently in a state of near-panic.
The *Mir-El-Lah* appeared to be encircled by jagged rocks, menacingly
black against the night sky. Jumping down into the engine-room hatch, I
threw the engine into reverse, taking the way off her. But it seemed an
eternity before she finally stopped. When I came back on deck San Lorenzo
had taken over the wheel and the *Mir-El-Lah* was rolling gently in a lazy
swell. We had been seconds away from a fatal collision. Cursing myself for
my carelessness, I stared at the rocks forming a semi-circle around us. I
called to Madeka to keep the engine in reverse and slowly – painfully slowly
– we went astern clear of the trap until San Lorenzo could swing the *Mir-El-
Lah*'s bows towards the open sea.

'*Mungo iko!*' I laughed with Madeka and Kimuyu. ('God is here'!)

We then drifted until daylight. There was no telling what other dangers
lay ahead. That morning I looked up the entry in the *Gulf Pilot* dealing with

the coast between Ras Marabat and Ras Qiunquari. It was only then that I fully realised how near we had come to disaster, for the *Pilot* warned that the coast was highly dangerous and dotted with isolated rocks, inhabited only by a few cave dwellers; the last place in the world one would wish to be shipwrecked.

That morning we headed for Salalah, the capital of Dhofar, where, as our friend the Sheikh had explained, there was a war going on between the mountain tribesmen and the Sultan of Oman. Dhofar borders on Yemen – the People's Republic of South Yemen. The rebels were communists fighting under the banner of PFLOAG – The Popular Front for the Liberation of the Occupied Arabian Gulf. Originally backed by the Chinese, they were now receiving arms from Russia. This complicated situation involved not only the People's Republic of South Yemen, but also the British, who were helping the Sultan and the Shah of Iran, who had sent an Irani expeditionary force to Oman.

There were no signs of civil war or revolution when we approached the oasis of Salalah. The *Pilot* mentioned that the cultivation in Salalah gave the coast a fresh green appearance from seaward; it did not prepare me for the great fields of alfalfa, the giant palms, coconut and banana groves, above which rose a fort, a large palace and a line of gracious old houses surrounded by flower gardens.

I had expected to sail into Salalah, but quickly realised no harbour existed, only a long beach on which the heavy surf was breaking. We continued a few miles down the coast to Bandar Risut, the new artificial harbour built around an existing rocky bluff two hundred feet high. As we entered it I was overjoyed to find we had finally caught up with the East African dhow fleet and, as we zig-zagged amongst the *sambuks* and *booms* in search of an anchorage, Madeka and Kimuyu shouted greetings as they sighted old friends from Dubai. 'Salama!' 'Jambo mingi!' 'Habari ya Salalah?' ('How are things in Salalah?').

Soon after we had dropped anchor a motor launch came alongside and a tall, good-looking Englishman came aboard. He introduced himself as the harbourmaster and told me our friend from Muscat, Sheikh Omer, had cabled him of our intended arrival. In spite of the war raging in the mountains, he said, things were peaceful in the town, where we would not be troubled by red tape and could buy provisions and wander around without harassment from officials.

I had no need to invite him to tea, for as soon as he came over the side Kimuyu was waiting with the tea-tray. His name was Jeremy. As we settled

Overleaf Mukhallah, in the Peoples Republic of South Yemen, where I ran into my worst political problem

down to our tea ritual, Kimuyu returned to his fishing. He lowered a small square net, baited with a boiled potato, over the side and in less than a minute, yelling with excitement, he hauled it up filled with glittering mackerel. When I expressed my amazement Jeremy smiled and said, 'The fishing here is fantastic.'

Jeremy was a mine of local information. He explained that this small section of the barren Arab Peninsula owed its lush vegetation to underground springs. These were fed by the water from the northern mountains, which seldom emerged from the clouds during the south-west monsoon and the high humidity. Later, when we went ashore with him, it was an enormous relief to find that the town was still unspoilt, and the stalls in its market well stocked with traditional merchandise instead of the usual Sony radios and plastic toys. As we wandered round the *souk* (bazaar) I found a magnificent old copper vase six feet tall and four feet wide, lying under inches of dust in the corner of a shop. I bought it for Mirella, but when we tried to take it away we found it could not go through the door or the windows. I can only think it must have been there a very long time. We had to call a mason to smash down part of a wall so that we could get it out.

Before we returned aboard, Jeremy took us to a lovely tropical garden surrounding the Sultan's palace. Amongst the trees were several bungalows originally built for slaves. Jeremy introduced us to one of them, the 'chamberlain' of the Wali. He told us sadly that he was now a free citizen and had had to work in order to provide for his old age. Had he still been a slave, he explained with a note of regret, the Wali would have provided for him for the rest of his life. 'The good old days are gone,' he said.

I was now on the last leg of my trip along the Arab Peninsula. After my next port of call, Mukhallah, in the People's Democratic Republic of South Yemen, I would cross over to Africa. Jeremy strongly advised me to avoid Mukhallah, but I explained it was too much a part of the world of the dhows to be ignored, and also that I had a rendezvous there with Mirella and my daughter Marina, who were arriving from India. I pointed out, too, that when I had called on the ambassador at the South Yemen Embassy in London I had been assured that we would be welcome in his country and would need no written permission or visas. The *Mir-El-Lah*, I explained, sailed under the Panamanian flag, and our Italian and Kenyan passports would ensure a friendly reception. Nevertheless, Jeremy's last words of advice were to sail well away from the land and enter Mukhallah from the high seas.

*

Everything went well for us on the three-hundred-mile passage to Mukhallah. On the first evening a tern landed on deck. It was a friendly bird and tame enough to be caressed. I took it as a good omen. Even Kimuyu, who had been sad at leaving Salalah, knowing he would never again catch so many fish, was cheered by our visitor.

The weather remained perfect, with a Force 3 to 4 north-easterly wind filling our sails. Not once did we experience the *belat*, the strong land wind common during that season along the coast of Arabia. The shaft had settled down, the water-pump had been forgotten, and the engine ran smoothly and quietly; gone were the days when I found myself sniffing around for fires. There was a wonderful atmosphere of peace and well-being as we came in sight of Mukhallah on the Hadhramaut coast.

I had taken my last bearing on the Arabian coast from Ras Fartak, a prominent cape halfway between Mukhallah and the South Yemen – Omani border, and my navigation was faultless. We hit the coast slightly north of the city, just as I had planned.

Overleaf The city of Mukhallah sprawls from the hills onto the beach

15. Prison

I had heard much about Mukhallah, but when I saw this fabled town it was even more beautiful than I had imagined. The white lace-like houses clustered at the foot of the mountains dated back to the days of the Queen of Sheba. To the north of the city tall thin white towers rose out of the red sandstone cliffs, while great ochre-coloured castles stood defiantly on the hilltops behind. It must have looked exactly the same to all the navigators of dhows who sailed there before me.

So entranced was I by my first sight of Mukhallah that I allowed a sudden gust of wind to snatch a chart from my hands and carry it away like a kite. Fortunately it was retrieved by a Customs boat that came out to meet us with two civilians and four soldiers on board.

As soon as we dropped anchor they boarded the *Mir-El-Lah*. Over tea and biscuits they plied me with questions: Where had I come from? Where was I going? What was I carrying? On an impulse I answered the first by saying I had sailed directly from Dubai, a falsehood which was to give me many anxious moments later, and probably saved our lives. Having examined my papers they departed politely, merely requesting us to remain on board until the following day, when we would be allowed on shore.

Contentedly we sat on deck watching the setting sun turn the lovely white city to rose red and listened to the *muezzin* call the faithful to prayer. We drank Kimuyu's Bajun *chai*, a special brew made of milk, sugar, water, tea leaves and cinnamon all boiled together: the lazy man's tea, and the perfect thing to drink before falling asleep under the stars.

I was wakened in the middle of the night by the sound of an approaching motor boat; by the time I was on my feet three armed soldiers were on deck.

'The captain, where is the captain?' one of them shouted.

'I am the captain,' I told him.

'Come with us,' he said. 'The harbourmaster wishes to speak to you.'

'At this hour?' I asked.

'Just come with us,' he insisted. 'You will soon be back.'

I did not like the tone of his voice, nor was I impressed by his appearance. He was wearing a nondescript army jacket, filthy grey trousers and Indian sandals. Certainly he did not convince me that he was an officer; a political commissar perhaps? I glanced at the service revolver stuck in his belt and followed him to his launch.

We landed by the Customs house, which was inside a compound surrounded by a wall. There the chief dismissed the three soldiers, and as one of them left he smiled and said in Italian, '*Arriverderci, amico*'; he was a Somali. Then the commissar motioned me to precede him through the main gate and into the city of Mukhallah. We made our way in single file down narrow alleys that stank until we came to a cemetery that seemed to me the perfect spot for a quick, clean murder. I thought of the revolver he was carrying and what I would do if he cornered me. If I tried to jump him, the chances were I would get shot in the back and, even if he missed me, any shot fired would attract attention.

I was still deliberating whether to play James Bond and hit him when he nudged me across a small square with his revolver and up the stone stairs of a high building. On one landing we passed a sentry squatting on his haunches and nursing his rifle. On the fourth floor my guard showed me into an unfurnished room and locked the door behind me. I was a prisoner.

There was an open window but it offered no way of escape. Below me lay a panoramic view of the harbour with the silhouette of the *Mir-El-Lah* at anchor, her riding-light swinging in the rigging. Why the long walk through all those alleyways? I asked myself. Slowly I realised that no harbourmaster wanted to see me. They had lied to get me ashore. What did they want with me? And who were 'they' anyway?

I was still asking myself such questions when I heard footsteps along the corridor. The door was unlocked and in came San Lorenzo, his inscrutable smile hiding his feelings.

'What the hell's going on?' I asked.

He shrugged. 'I don't know. Half an hour after you left they came back for me.'

'Soon they'll bring Kimuyu and Madeka,' I told him, crossing to the window. 'They're searching the *Mir-El-Lah* now. Come and look!'

There was a launch alongside her and I could just make out figures moving on the deck, some with torches flashing.

'Do you realise what this means with what we have on board? Mirella's cameras and exposed films, my guns, the diving gear, a long-range walkie-talkie, a radio. They've got enough evidence to shoot us as spies!' I told him.

San Lorenzo shrugged. 'They don't need any of that to incriminate us. If they're really after us, all they have to do is plant on board a little hash or

Overleaf Myself (*right*) with a *nakhoda* from Mukhallah.
'A man with a beard like yours is a real man,' he told
me, and offered me hospitality on his *sambuk*

cocaine – or maybe a couple of cases of machine-guns.'

He was right. They could do what they liked with us and we were completely at their mercy. I had lied to them by saying we had sailed direct from Dubai; if they checked up, they would be sure we were spies. Spies or not, they had a war on their hands, and the Yemeni were poor and fanatical. The *Mir-El-Lah* and the equipment aboard were worth at least £30,000 – and she was there for the taking.

'No one knows where we are,' I said. 'I told Jeremy we were coming to Mukhallah. But who will ever know if we got here? These fellows can kill us and sail *Mir-El-Lah* anywhere. No-one would ever know what had happened to us.'

'Don't worry,' said San Lorenzo. '*Dio vede e provvede.*' ('God sees and provides'.) The Italian version of *Allah karim*.

At that moment the door was opened and Kimuyu and Madeka were pushed into the room, wide-eyed and trembling.

'The best thing we can do is get some sleep,' San Lorenzo said.

I slept soundly as I always do in a crisis.

At about seven in the morning the commissar came into our room. Telling the others to stay where they were, he escorted me across the hall to another small room where three men sat at a desk armed with ball-point pens, writing-pads and maps. They were short, hairy, thickset fellows wearing Indonesian *sarongs*, European shirts and plastic Chinese sandals; they looked as though they were dressed for a *ngoma* (dance) rather than officials of a people's republic. Waving me to a chair, one of them addressed me in Swahili and the other two in excellent English.

Then began an interrogation that lasted six hours. From the start I knew I must keep my wits and my temper, for when they were through with me they would question San Lorenzo, Kimuyu and Madeka separately; obviously I must stick to my original statement that we had sailed direct from Dubai to Mukhallah – the others had heard me say so; but, while I was quite sure they would not trip San Lorenzo, I was far from certain that Kimuyu and Madeka could survive their cross-examination.

Their questions went on and on. Where were you born? Three years ago what were you doing? How long have you owned your dhow? When were you married? Where is your wife? Why is she not travelling with you? How many children have you? Then, suddenly, had I seen the green valley of Salalah? They popped that in every now and again and every time I answered 'no', but I had a feeling they did not believe me.

Struggling not to lose my temper I told them that if they wished to confirm my story all they had to do was to get in touch with my wife and daughter, who were staying in Aden as guests of the British High Commissioner. This lie seemed to impress them.

'Why not send my wife a cable telling her where we are?' I suggested. 'They are waiting for us and will be worried if we don't turn up.' Their expressions told me nothing as they scribbled their notes.

To my consternation, when I was returned to our room San Lorenzo, Madeka and Kimuyu had been taken away. I had hoped for a chance to whisper 'Remember we sailed to Mukhallah non-stop from Dubai.' Now they were probably being interrogated in separate rooms and frightened out of their lives. Out of the window I saw the *Mir-El-Lah* riding peacefully at anchor – but at least two dozen soldiers were now on board.

One by one San Lorenzo, Madeka and Kimuyu came back. They were followed by a soldier armed with a revolver, who settled himself on a chair and warned us that we must not talk to each other. We spent the rest of the day sitting on the filthy floor staring at the walls of our prison; the only indication of the passing time was the three-hourly changing of our guard.

Round about dawn, two hours after the sentry had been changed, I noticed that our guard had fallen asleep on the floor; his gun lay on the chair beside him. I grabbed it, woke San Lorenzo and gestured to the boys to keep quiet. They shook their heads violently, thinking I was going to shoot the guard. I had a better plan. I nudged him, clutching the gun in my hands. He woke slowly, staring at me in terror. Before he could say anything, I handed the gun back to him and, guessing he was a Somali, spoke to him in Italian. 'If your commander had caught you asleep and without your gun you would have been shot. Keep it and stay awake,' I told him, smiling at him. My plan worked. He grinned at me and opened the breech, showing me the pistol was empty. Then, having decided that, even if I was a spy, I was a friend, he whispered a long tirade against the Yemeni communists. They were the biggest bastards in the world, he told us, and they had made the country bankrupt; he and the rest of the Somali volunteers had not been paid for months. Everyone hated the Yemeni communists' guts. On his knees he begged me to help him escape to Somalia. He told me all this in a whisper in Italian, using all his verbs in the infinitive as is typical of the Somalis.

Once our relationship had been established and I had gained his confidence, my plan unfolded. I told him I would be happy to take him to Somaliland as we were going there, providing he could come without risk of being shot as a deserter. But, first, we had to be released. Then I asked who had imprisoned us. Spitting on the floor, he told me we were in the hands of

Overleaf Mogadishu, the capital of Somalia

the secret police and that the official authorities probably did not know of our existence. As for himself, he was just a simple soldier and had to do whatever the secret police officers ordered.

As usual, I had some money hidden in my belt. I put three ten-dollar bills into his hand. 'I want you to take this man,' I said, pointing to Madeka, 'into the town so that he can send a telegram. Give one ten-dollar bill to your superior; say it is to buy food for us. When you come back with the receipts for the telegrams I will give you another twenty dollars.'

Hassan, for that was his name, agreed immediately.

I knew we had not long before he would be relieved by another sentry so I wrote my telegrams quickly: one to the British High Commissioner in Aden and one to Mirella's family in Kenya – all carefully worded in case the post office should pass them to the secret police.

After the guard had been changed, an hour passed before Hassan opened the door and called to Madeka to come with him. The new guard watched them go but said nothing. Neither did he seem surprised when Hassan returned to take over his duty followed by Madeka, carrying a large carton of food, and handed over to me the receipts for my telegrams.

'Thank you, Hassan,' I said, pressing another twenty dollars into his hand and suspecting that he had more than doubled his year's pay in a few hours.

For the rest of his spell of duty, we listened to his eulogy of the Italians. He told us how Somalia had gone down the drain since the Italians' departure. '*Si stava meglio quando si stava peggio*' – 'We were better off when we were worse off,' he repeated, a well-known phrase. 'And the Italians were such good people.' Finally, with tears in his eyes, he begged us to arrange for our countrymen to return. Poor Hassan, he had given us good value. He explained that we were imprisoned in the Mukhallah Hotel and, as he had had to give the cable office a return address, we could expect our friend the commissar to intercept the replies to our wires.

Two days later the head of the secret police called on us, accompanied by several henchmen. Pretending that he could not speak English or Italian, he kept waving a telegram as if it were a fan, while one of the others explained it had just arrived from Aden. Then, dropping it on the floor, he departed with his entourage. As the door slammed behind them, I picked it up. It was from Mirella and it read: 'Stay where you are. Sorting problems Aden. Time of arrival Mukhallah uncertain.' I liked the 'Stay where you are' bit.

From that moment on we saw no more of the secret police; all the guards, including Hassan, were removed, and the commissar advised us that we were to remain in the hotel at our own expense until our friends arrived. In the meantime we would not be allowed to return to the *Mir-El-Lah* which, he assured me, was being guarded against thieves by a large company of soldiers. *Quis custodiet custodem?* ('Who guards the guards?')

That same afternoon a young man presented himself as the official guide of our party, saying he had been detailed to show us round Mukhallah. We accepted eagerly, because it was an opportunity not only to leave the four depressing walls of our room, but also to see the legendary city at last.

In a square we came across some sort of political meeting at which a young Yemeni on a rostrum was declaiming the Marxist doctrine to a captive audience of old men and women, school girls and boys. Half of the women were still wearing their traditional face masks, the other half were dressed in shoddy Western clothes. All were chanting the set slogans, parrot-fashion, and appeared as apathetic as the orator was passionate, clearly demonstrating that it takes more than mere oratory to arouse an Arab crowd under the heat of the midday sun.

Mirella and Marina arrived the following day in a battered old DC3 of the Yemeni Airways. They brought with them a letter for San Lorenzo recalling him to London. Before departing he told me I had added to his life one of those never-to-be-forgotten moments.

To our enormous relief, when we returned to the *Mir-El-Lah* we found that although she had been thoroughly searched nothing had been stolen. Aboard, to my delight, I found Hassan, for I had feared for his life. Sadly he told me he dared not come with us for, if he deserted, his wife and two children would suffer. He asked me what route we would be taking, and when I told him our next step would be Ras Hafun he shook his head.

'Ras Hafun! But there is nothing in Ras Hafun. No fuel. No nothing.'

I pointed out that my *Pilot* said it was a well-stocked port on the Somali coast. 'No need to look at your book, I am telling you, sir!' He embraced me and said I must sail direct to Mogadishu.

Mukhallah to Mogadishu is one thousand miles, and Lamu four hundred miles further; so before leaving Mukhallah I bought six drums of diesel oil, which I lashed on deck, enough to take us to Kenya without refuelling. Possible stop-overs were the island of Soccotra, Abdal Kuri and The Brothers; but in Mukhallah I had been warned to give them a wide berth, expecially Soccotra, which was now a Russian submarine base and out of bounds to everyone. North of Kenya, the East African coast has not a single harbour in which one can seek shelter – Mogadishu has only a small artificial harbour silted up for lack of dredging. I therefore had no choice but to plan on making for Lamu direct.

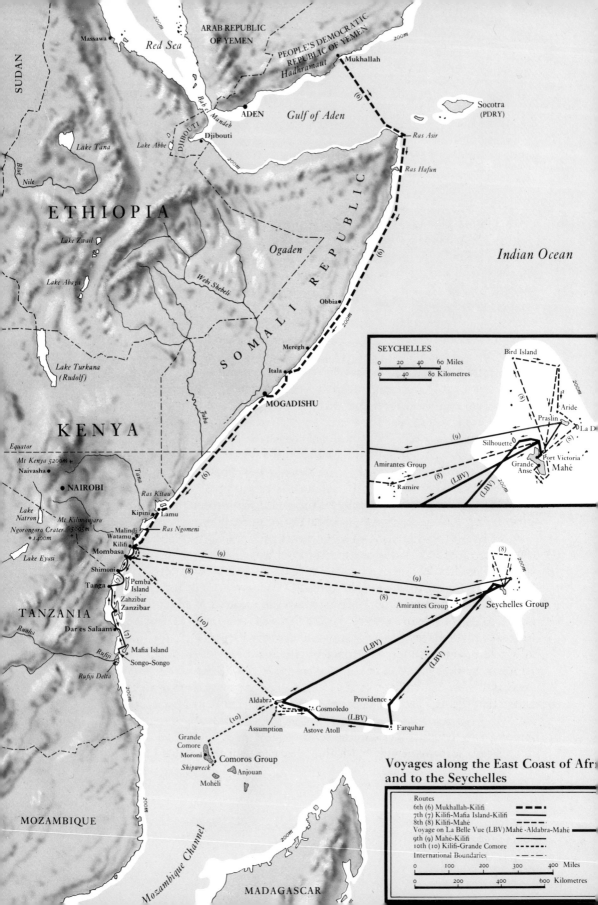

SUDAN

Massawa

Red Sea

ARAB REPUBLIC
OF YEMEN

PEOPLE'S DEMOCRATIC
REPUBLIC OF YEMEN
Hadhramaut   Mukhallah

200m

Bab el Mandeb
ADEN   *Gulf of Aden*   Socotra
                                                  (PDRY)
DJIBOUTI
Djibouti   Ras Asir

Lake Tana   (6)
                                                Ras Hafun
Lake Abbe

*Blue
Nile*

ETHIOPIA

Lake Zwai   *Indian Ocean*

Ogaden

Lake Abaya   S   Obbia

                             O
Lake Turkana   M
(Rudolf)   A   Meregh
                             L   *Webi Shebeli*
                             I   Itala
                             Juba
KENYA   R
                             E   MOGADISHU
                             P
Equator   U
Mt Kenya 5200m   B   (6)
Naivasha   L
                             I
NAIROBI   C   SEYCHELLES

Lake   *Tana*   0 20 40 60 Miles   Bird Island
Natron   Mt Kilimanjaro   0   40   80 Kilometres
Ngorongoro Crater 5895m   Ras Kitau   (8)
1400m   Kipini Lamu   2
Lake Eyasi   Malindi   Ras Ngomeni   Praslin Aride
             Watamu   La D
TANZANIA   Kilifi   Silhouette   (9)
             Mombasa   (9)   Amirantes Group   (8)
     Shimoni   (8)   Grande Port Victoria
Tanga   Pemba   Anse   Mahé
            Island   (9)
Zanzibar   (8)   (8)
Ruaha Zanzibar   Amirantes Group   Seychelles Group
Dar es Salaam   (10)
         Mafia Island (7)
Rufiji Songo-Songo   (LBV)
Rufiji Delta   (LBV)
                                                    Aldabra   Providence
                              (10)   Cosmoledo
                                                         (LBV)
                     Assumption   Astove Atoll   Farquhar
                Grande
                Comore
                Moroni   Comoros Group   **Voyages along the East Coast of Afr**
MOZAMBIQUE   *Shipwreck*   Anjouan   **and to the Seychelles**
                     Moheli
                                              Routes
                                              6th (6) Mukhallah-Kilifi
                                              7th (7) Kilifi-Mafia Island-Kilifi
                                              8th (8) Kilifi-Mahé
                                              Voyage on La Belle Vue (LBV)Mahé-Aldabra-Mahé
                                              9th (9) Mahé-Kilifi
                                              10th (10) Kilifi-Grande Comore
                                              International Boundaries
                     MADAGASCAR   0   100   200   300   400 Miles
                                              0   200   400   600 Kilometres

16. Africa

The monsoon was still holding when we left Mukhallah, but I had an uncomfortable feeling that it would not last much longer and that it would be followed by shifting winds and rains alternating with flat calms. At four in the morning I set a course for Ras Asir (Cape Guardafui), the Horn of Africa. The passage of two hundred miles was easy; the only problem being to distinguish Ras Asir from Capo Elefante when out at sea in hazy weather. In fact, I spent the whole night peering into the blackness searching in vain for the beam from the lighthouse of Guardafui, and it was not until daylight that I picked up Ras Asir through my binoculars. Triumphant, I called to Madeka and Kimuyu somewhat theatrically: 'Brothers,' I said, 'we are in Africa. This is your country; I have brought you home!'

As I looked at this famous landmark the story of the 'Prince of Guardafui' came to my mind. It dates back to the days when Somalia was an Italian colony. The 'Prince' was the lighthouse keeper who had worked on that barren rock for many years in solitude and had saved up a tidy sum of money. But the burning sun, the fierce winds and the loneliness had turned his head. At the age of fifty-five he decided to get married. He went to Mogadishu and despatched an advertisement to the *Popolo d'Italia* in Rome in which, proclaiming himself Prince of Guardafui, he stated that he was seeking a young bride to share his castle in the lovely hills of Ras Asir. No fewer than nine hopefuls arrived in Mogadishu – and discovered the bleak truth; the 'Prince' fled back to his lighthouse as fast as he could and continued his solitary life until he committed a spectacular suicide by jumping two thousand feet into the sea.

I hoisted the mainsail and jib, wishing I had a mizzen mast so that I could set more canvas to save fuel and to speed the *Mir-El-Lah* southwards. Our passage, in the best tradition of Arab dhows, became a race with the wind. By night I steered a course to seaward, and with the dawn headed towards the coast to check my position as best I could; but it was not easy as the Somali coastline is flat with few landmarks. I did not venture very near to Ras Hafun or Dante, though I was close enough inshore to see that the former was now little more than a pile of rubble.

Further down the coast we passed close to a Somali offshore oil rig. We waved to her crew, but this was returned with sullen stares. Then they chased after us in a motor launch, waving their arms, shouting at us in Arabic to get the hell out of there. In return I shouted back, '*Ibn al sharmut!*' ('Son of a bitch'), angrily brandishing my .22 rifle. Soon after, we were buzzed several times by a twin-engined Russian aircraft.

After that brief encounter many days passed during which we did not sight another vessel. To starboard the featureless, undulating sand dunes of the Somali coast stretched for mile upon mile looking always the same. Kimuyu and Madeka were happy, spending their waking hours hauling in fish as fast as they could cast their lines. At times I joined them, my feathered Japanese jigs hooking a fish every two or three minutes, until Mirella intervened and insisted that the massacre should stop.

We were often less than a quarter of a mile off the coast and now and again spotted a camel caravan, the odd herd of gazelles and a few nomadic fishermen, so completely isolated that we wondered how they survived in such a bleak environment.

After the seventh day at sea the monsoon turned; if the *Mir-El-Lah* had been engineless, I would probably never have made the Kenya coast. The *nakhodas* who had left ahead of us told me later that I had sailed a month too late on this historic run from the Shatt-al-Arab to Africa. My situation was not improved by the fact that I had miscalculated the amount of fuel I would need to make Mogadishu, and had only a vague idea of my position.

But after sailing south for another day Allah came to my rescue in the shape of a small fishing vessel with four men aboard. We hailed them and threw them cans of tinned food as they came alongside. They spoke neither Italian nor English, but I shouted the names of every village in the coastal area at them; they recognised 'Olbia' and managed to indicate that we had already passed it.

From the *Pilot* I read that the next port of any size was Itala, which '... has a light, a large castle and a palm grove which gives the appearance of an oasis ... provisions are scarce and the water somewhat brackish'.

We drifted south all night without sighting any of the beacons mentioned in the *Pilot*, until I began to wonder if Itala still existed or had crumbled into decay, its ruins overwhelmed by the desert. When daylight came, still clutching the *Pilot*, I sailed as close inshore as I dared, checking every possible landmark, every hill, headland, lone tree. At last I picked up the Massawa beacon, a cylindrical pillar surmounted by a pole ten metres high and painted black and white as described, standing on a dune two cables westward of the Residency of Meregh. At last I knew my position.

We reached Itala that evening, with hardly any fuel left. Its light, thank God, was working, and the moon was bright. Rather than risk negotiating the reef we anchored outside it in a flat calm. Hundreds of sooty terns welcomed us, landing on our heads and shoulders; their boldness was such that we had to swat them away like flies. One of the more insistent kept landing on Madeka's fuzzy head while he was grappling with the anchor rope; another perched on my shoulder and came with me over the side into the dinghy.

Towards midnight the wind freshened, bringing with it a long uneasy swell. One of our anchor ropes fouled the rudder post and I had to dive to free it. It was an eerie experience swimming in the murky water holding a torch that cast a sinister yellow light, keeping a constant look out for sharks. It was nearly dawn before I freed the rope and climbed back aboard in time to watch the birds take flight like small vampires afraid of the rising sun.

Early that morning Madeka and I took off in the dinghy to reconnoitre the channels through the reef and find a safe passage for the *Mir-El-Lah* at high tide. I was anxious to anchor inside the reef so that we could sleep protected from the swell. We soon found a deep channel that enabled me to drop two anchors within a couple of hundred yards of the beach. Our unexpected arrival quickly attracted a large crowd, who came running across the white sand and gathered round us as we waded ashore from the dinghy. They were very beautiful people, with Nilotic features and honey-coloured skin; the women wore long, colourful billowing clothes, the men *kikois* wrapped round their strong lean bodies. Amongst them were three or four uniformed guards with rifles, one of whom greeted me in English and seemed pleased when I answered him in Italian.

He led us to a house where we were immediately offered food and drinks, and the local schoolmaster welcomed us in the name of the village. Meanwhile, the sergeant began a long telephone conversation in Somali. When it ended he said, 'Now they will come.'

'Who?' I asked, a little alarmed.

Overleaf Returning to the Gulf. In the distance is the coast of Somalia

'The police,' he replied.

'Why did you call the police? I'm not staying. All I want is to buy some drums of diesel for my dhow and be on my way to Mogadishu,' I explained.

'But I am under orders to call them if anything unusual happens. You happened, you are unusual, so I call them. If I don't call them, they shoot me,' he said flatly.

'Can I buy fuel in the meantime?'

'No, you must wait until they come.'

'Where are they coming from?'

'Mogadishu.'

'But that's miles away! It will take them several days.'

The sergeant smiled, spreading his hands. 'Don't worry, you will see – they will come. We will look after you.'

It was no use getting angry. The poor devil was only doing his duty. If he let us go, or if I made a dash for it, they would probably shoot him. I began to suspect that we were in for another Mukhallah version of Marxist hospitality.

However, it was some consolation that the sergeant was clearly unhappy at having to keep us under guard and did his best to make us comfortable in a two-roomed bungalow, sparsely furnished with a few chairs, a table and three beds with thin mattresses and, thank God, clean sheets. We were plied with more food and drink than we could manage and were free to wander where we liked, so long as we stayed in the town and did not take photographs. The schoolmaster even produced an accordion, which I proceeded to play to the delight of the local children.

Had it not been for my worries about the shifting monsoon, Mirella and I could easily have enjoyed a few weeks in Itala with its snow-white beaches and beautiful people. But on the fourth day, when 'they' – the political agents – arrived, I had almost reached the limit of my patience. 'Their' appearance did nothing to reassure me, for they seemed to have been created in the same mould as our Yemeni interrogators. Yet, somehow, I felt I was in no real danger now and decided on a radically different approach when they started questioning me.

I was, I assured them, in my right mind and lived by sailing my dhow round the world.

'And your occupation?'

'A spy.'

'A spy?' they exclaimed. 'What do you mean?'

'I am a spy of nature. I spy on the rising sun and the setting sun. I spy on

On the beach at Itala in Somalia with some friends. They gave me
an accordion and *spaghetti al pomodoro*

nature at sea, under the sea, and on land. I spy on the lovely faces of your
people, and I am a happy man.'

They gaped at me, not knowing whether to take me seriously, to get angry
or to laugh. At the end of that hour of interrogation I am certain they were
convinced I was a madman – but a harmless one!

'Buy your fuel,' they told me, 'then go away!'

Helped by a laughing band of children, we rolled the oil-drums over the
sand into the water and floated them out to the *Mir-El-Lah*, and we finally
set sail at midnight.

Twenty-four hours later we were off Mogadishu. Three large steamers
were unloading their cargoes into lighters, rolling in the heavy swell off the
harbour. I knew that for want of dredging the harbour had silted up, but as it

was high water I decided to take advantage of the *Mir-El-Lah*'s shallow draught rather than remain out at sea. The harbour was a depressing sight for it was rapidly falling into decay. It would have taken very little maintenance to keep it in good shape, for the Italians had constructed it with care and expertise.

The news that a madman was bound for Mogadishu had preceded us, and when the police came aboard they were as kind and understanding as nurses in an asylum. I was wearing my white *dish-dash* and a red-and-white-check turban tied in the Omani fashion, with my splendid *khanjar* strapped round my waist. As I welcomed them with a thunderous '*Salaam aleikum*' I felt I was living up to my reputation.

During our two-day stay in Mogadishu, I spread the word that I was a Moslem, and wherever we went in the city curious crowds followed. Others gathered on the quayside, staring down at the *Mir-El-Lah* flying her strange, colourful flag, so that I felt had I stayed longer I would have been taken for one of Allah's prophets. I dressed Madeka and Kimuyu in plain beige *dish-dashes* and white Irani turbans, and the rumour quickly spread that they were my disciples. They reported to me that within twenty-four hours of our arrival I was no longer looked upon as a madman but as a saintly stranger sailing the seven seas in search of truth. Since I could speak about ten phrases in Arabic, all of which – bar one – invoked Allah, I must have given a convincing performance as I wandered along the boulevards of the city. It had, I noticed, absorbed many of the charms of my native land, with its open-air cafés and restaurants, its market full of fresh fruits and vegetables; in some of its shops we still found Italian shopkeepers selling *panettone, salami, prosciutto, pane* and *chianti*.

Finally, to the relief of the police and the sorrow of our followers, the wild-eyed 'Prophet' boarded his dhow *Emir Allah* – 'God is king' – and sailed away into the sunset.

As if to punish me for my tardiness the monsoon now turned against me, growing in anger every day until, just as we reached the Somali – Kenya border, it struck us with all its might. I had closed into the land to get my bearings and when I altered course to seaward the gale-force wind struck us head-on, bringing with it driving rain squalls. To make matters worse, we were in the area of the Pazarli Rocks, notorious for its menacing coral reefs, some of which extended three miles off shore. Although I knew the coast well, under such conditions navigation was a nightmare; but for my powerful engine we would have been driven broadside on to the rocks. I could clearly hear the heavy seas breaking against them.

The sun suddenly broke through the clouds, briefly playing on the wreck of a Greek cargo ship which for years had been rusting on the outer Kiunga Reef, and at last I knew where I was. But my relief was brief, for just as I ordered Madeka to put the engine to full throttle thick black smoke began to pour from the exhaust. There was a lot of sand in that fuel from Itala and it was silting up the engine.

I had no alternative but to keep going and head into the seas, praying I could keep steerage-way at full speed. For the next three hours I played this desperate tug-of-war against the monsoon, always watching the palm trees on the shore to make sure I was holding my own. My diesel consumption during this battle doubled, and I began to fear we would run out of fuel. So I had Madeka and Kimuyu double the anchor ropes and make ready the extra-heavy dhow-anchor I had retrieved from the seabed off Musandam. Then, just as I was getting really worried, I noticed that the *Mir-El-Lah* was moving slowly, very slowly, ahead. We were still not out of danger and still had to fight our way out of Puta Bay and avoid the reef. I knew I would only feel safe when I sighted the sand dunes of Lamu, the pillars of Shella lighthouse and the iron beacons at the entrance to the bay. It was vital that we reach Lamu before nightfall, and it was already late in the afternoon. Nature had unleashed against me the full strength of the monsoon combined with an incoming tide. Every now and again, between the rain squalls, I caught sight of the palm trees on the coastal hills and at last saw that we were gaining ground. Sometimes the hills seemed familiar, then suddenly I could not recognise them at all.

As the sun was sinking below the horizon, I finally sighted the pillars of Lamu. I recognised Shella Channel, and opposite to the Peponi Hotel, Manda Island. We rounded Ras Kitau and suddenly we were sailing before the wind again. I switched off the engine, leaving the lateen sail to carry us up the channel. Mirella tied several of her multi-coloured *kikois* to a rope and hoisted them together with all the flags of the countries we had visited on our 4,500-mile voyage: Iran, Dubai, Oman, Yemen, Somali and, of course, there was also the flag of the Sultan of Panama.

It was the magic hour, the first hour of twilight in the tropics, when the sky turns rose pink and the sea a deep blue. We sailed slowly past a few *jahazis* (coastal dhows) and fishing canoes towards the village of Lamu, where we dropped our anchors.

I went forward and sat down by the bows with Mirella, Marina, Madeka and Kimuyu. We were a family group and did not really want anyone else around for at least a little while.

PART THREE

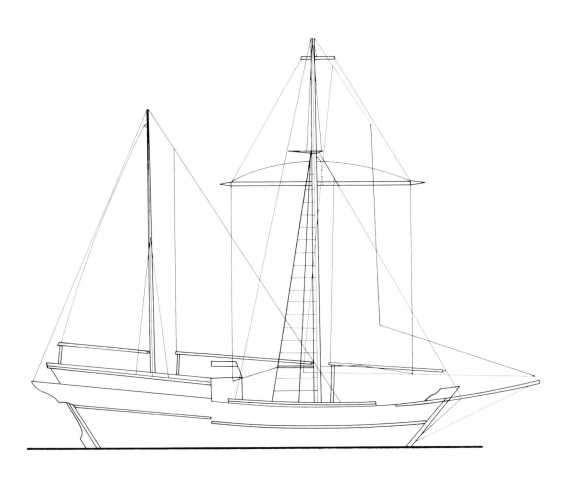

17. The Big Fish

My joy and relief on reaching Lamu almost overwhelmed me. I was now in home waters, the coastline and sea were familiar. My crew was home too: those two African brothers of mine, Madeka and Kimuyu, had disappeared, but I knew where to find them – with the Lamu *bints* (girls).

My family had returned to enjoy normal life again in our house at Kilifi, and in the evening I found myself alone on board. I sat on the poop reciting Dante's words aloud: '. . . *era gia l'ora che volge il disio ai naviganti e intenerisce il core lo di che han detto ai dolci amici addio.*' ('It was the time when sailors feel homesick and the heart softens as they remember when they said farewell to their dear friends.')

Our arrival had coincided with the celebration of Maulidis, a Moslem religious festival, which drew inhabitants from the surrounding islands and settlements to Lamu. The men were all dressed in white, the women in black *buibuis*. Small Lamu *jahazis* were approaching from all sides with their lateen sails spread. Lamu is an island in a maze of shallow canals, a flat piece of land surrounded by mangrove swamps, looking like the site of Venice before its construction; from the air, or on a nautical chart, one can see what a marvellous Chinese puzzle could be made from the Bajun Islands. The inhabitants too are made up of fragments of all sorts of people: in Lamu, as in the Musandam Peninsula, one sees that the Arabs, the Portuguese, the Indians have been blending with the Africans for centuries.

Lamu, my sailors told me, is known as a place for hot-blooded women, a place where passion and stifling heat mingle easily with aphrodisiacs. It is a hot place for lusty sailors who, after drinking the local *pombe* (beer), find it difficult to tell a young boy from an old virgin – not that they would really care. That old Italian sailor Pino, from the days of my boat *Samaki*, used to say, '*Dove ci sono campane, ci sono puttane*' – 'Where there are church bells there are whores'. Here, instead of bells, we had the hi-fi *muezzins* blasting out their taped prayers from tall loudspeakers once known as minarets.

But at last I was on my own. When I awoke next morning I felt like a fighter pilot whose war had ended.

Suddenly I wanted to get home to Kilifi, one day's sailing down the coast.

Madeka and Kimuyu had returned on board with many friends, including
Simba, a *nakhoda*. So when I sailed I had a crew of nine volunteers led by
Simba, and I played for a while the distant role of ship-owner, allowing
everything to happen as if I were not on board. Simba tied the sail to the
boom with straw strings in such a way that when the boom reached the top
of the mast the sail could be set by breaking the strings and allowing the
wind to whip-crack it open. It was in this way that the Red Sea pirates made
their quick get-aways. A sheep's carcass dangled from the mast, and Kimuyu
was soon slicing off hunks of meat to make a Bajun kebab for everybody.

We sailed past Ziwayu and caught the smell of hundreds of sharks left to
dry on the rocks by local fishermen. At Kipini, where the Tana river joins
the sea, we cut through Formosa Bay to within sight of Ras Ngomeni and
Malindi; Vasco da Gama Point, off Watamu, was already dark and we could
see the lights of Blue Lagoon and Turtle Bay. The full moon lit our way
until we picked up the light of Kilifi and sailed past it to reach the *mlango*
(passage) through the reef. We lined up on the two entrance-beacons,
brought the sail down and entered the creek.

I could see my home now, with its green shutters; a light glowed from the
living-room. I anchored twenty feet from the majestic baobab tree growing
on my beach, against the corals which hold the foundations of my house.

We quickly unloaded our souvenirs – copper trays, pots, pans and vases –
whispering instructions in the moonlight to the background ripple of the
flowing tide. The line of volunteers passed the objects from hand to hand
and laid them down beneath the baobab. My younger daughter, Amina, sat
on the steps leading down to the beach, her arms hugging her knees, her
head on one side, a mischievous look on her face.

People began to arrive: friends, fishermen I knew, Combo, Juma, Ben,
Jengo. I sat with them on the beach and we shared a 'joint' as we looked at
the *Mir-El-Lah* lit by the moon in the safest anchorage she had had in
months. This was happiness, the perfect moment perhaps to die. Who owns
that beautiful vessel moored there? I wondered. Where has she come from?
If *only* I could board her and sail her myself one day . . .

In April when the winds change there can be spells of beautiful weather, the
most beautiful of the year. On one such day I set off for Mombasa with a
merry group of twelve of my compatriots from Milan who had chartered the
Mir-El-Lah. We hugged the reef and trawled four lines. I had Kimuyu and
Madeka on board as well as Juma, a new recruit. On the way we caught five
bonitos and a kingfish. I hoisted the bright-coloured Panamanian flag which

had a very close link with Mirella. Her grandfather, Phillippe Bunau-Varilla, had engineered the creation of the Republic of Panama. His wife had stitched together the first flag of the new Republic in a room of the Waldorf Astoria in 1905.

After five happy hours we entered the old port and dropped anchor under the ramparts of Fort Jesus alongside other dhows. I took my papers and went to pay a formal visit to Ali Sururu, the dhow harbourmaster of the old port. I climbed the wooden steps of the Customs house and walked in over dozens of carpets strewn all over the floor. They had been landed from the Persian dhows at anchor there and were being valued by the Customs official before being sold in Mombasa. My friend Atim, a merchant from Hodeida, was handling a huge bundle of Kenyan banknotes and counting them out to a *nakhoda* sitting on an old, brass-studded Arab chest. 'Salaam aleikums' and '*Aleikum salaams*' began flowing back and forth. Ali was in his office and at first did not recognise me – so many *nakhodas* go in and out of there every day. He stared at me, got up and said, '*Salamia mingi sana*' ('Very many greetings'), changing from Arabic to Swahili.

In five minutes my papers were cleared, and I told Ali that the *Mir-El-Lah* was going on to Shimoni, Tanga, Zanzibar, Dar-es-Salaam and the Seychelles. 'Any cargo?' he asked. 'Yes,' I replied, 'dreams.' Ali is a dhow man, a practical man; he looked at me and said, 'You *mazungu* [foreigners], you have too much money. You can afford to carry dreams for nothing, but I would rather fill your hold with salt and make a profit.'

Next morning at sunrise we sailed for Shimoni – and struck a reef. It was a clear case of over-confidence; I knew the place too well and had become careless. The vessel suddenly shuddered and leaned slightly to port, darting forward with a fifty-ton momentum that carried her further on to the reef. Madeka reacted quickly, motioning me over to the left to darker water, while Kimuyu slowed down the engine and shifted the gear into neutral. I heard the bottom of the *Mir-El-Lah* scrape the reef, but there were no sounds of wood-splintering cracks. Then the keel slid on to something solid and the bows seemed to point skyward for a few seconds. I thought it was the end; but the bow went down and we sailed on into the blue water again: we had jumped clear of the reef. The tide was rising, and the strength of the hull, combined with our great speed, had carried the dhow safely past the other side of Mombasa reef.

Later on we dropped anchor and I dived with my aqualung to inspect the damage. The keel had struck and slid its way through a decaying coral. In some parts it was finely chafed to the bare wood where the paint and

Overleaf I sailed many times from the Takaungu reef to Kilifi and learned to handle a lateen rig

anti-fouling had worn off; it looked as if some giant hand had scraped the hull with a wire brush. But there were no leaks; the elasticity of the wood had absorbed the impact very well. Kimuyu and Madeka smiled sheepishly at me and shook their heads. I, the *nakhoda*, smiled bravely back, but inside I was shaken to the core.

We reached Shimoni, an area of many islets and outlying reefs, at four in the afternoon and dropped anchor by Pemba Channel Fishing Club. Marlin fishing is good in the Pemba Channel and I had been there many times with my fishing boat *Samaki*. Across the channel the high green island of Pemba is now under Chinese control and is strictly out of bounds. Two gun-boats had often captured fishing cruisers from Kenya and had released their occupants only after lengthy diplomatic squabbles. I was possibly the first dhow for many years to use these waters, which had been closed since the Zanzibar revolution when the Arabs ceded their foothold in the spice island and thousands had lost their lives.

We went on to Tanga in Tanzania through the maze of shallow reefs that surrounded the harbour. My navigational capabilities were severely strained and I gave up trying to mark my position on the chart with my position in the water. I put Kimuyu at the wheel, cut the speed down to four

The *Mir-El-Lah* anchored beneath our house in Kilifi. Amina is beside a fish trap; behind her a giant baobab tree grows in the coral

knots and sat with Madeka in the bows, peering into the greenish-brown coastal waters.

I announced my arrival to the Tanzanian Navy, telling them I wished to proceed to Zanzibar. They agreed to phone their base there and told me I was welcome in their country and that my Tanzanian visa was also good for Zanzibar. However, it appeared that the line to Zanzibar was not good, and in any case they told me it did not really matter: '*Shauri ya mungu*' – 'It's God's business.'

Tanga is a sleepy town reflecting the moderate splendours of its colonial past. I was told I could not go ashore wearing shorts and would I please cut my hair a little. I immediately set sail for Zanzibar, eighty miles away.

The first part of the trip was free from hidden dangers so I decided to motor slowly by night and enjoy the peace. I had sighted several lighthouses and hoped I would be able to fix my position by consulting the pilot books; however, the time of each flashing light seemed to differ from the description given. I kept guessing and watching, and when day dawned I sighted the lighthouse at the northern tip of Zanzibar. We passed it and came to a white shady beach fringed by palm trees, standing out in the crisp morning light against the sapphire blue of the sea.

I dropped anchor just off the beach and we all went swimming around the dhow. Soon I saw Madeka waving to me to come back and pointing to a fast boat approaching from the south. A grey naval patrol boat came alongside and the usual tedious interrogation began. They told me to follow them to Zanzibar town; I said I was going there anyway. They asked why, and I replied that I had been there on honeymoon and was suffering from nostalgia. Who were all these people? And why did I have no cargo? I felt like saying that it was so that I should not be bothered by people like themselves, but I merely said we were tourists, rich enough not to have to carry a cargo. They were obviously suspicious, wondering why, in that case, I should be working as a *nakhoda*.

I decided it would be easier to terminate this conversation by following my captors to Zanzibar. We sailed along a deep underwater trench which follows the western contours of the island about a hundred yards from the shore. The town of Zanzibar does not have a proper harbour, but the waters there are sheltered by coral reefs and small islets.

Within minutes of our arrival I was submerged by a tide of politics. Teams of officials swarmed on board: Customs officers, intelligence officers, naval officers, immigration officials, medical officers, political officers, stupid officers and curious officers, each group claiming the right to seize our

Overleaf Sailing at three knots to Mombasa

passports. One lot were 'the preventative officers for the smuggling of cloves', and their leader hinted that there might be packages dangling from the keel. I suggested they should dive in and look, and a volunteer diver was called for. It appeared that nobody could swim, let alone dive. Having lost face, the leader decided to believe me and hurried his group away.

After a day of receiving and dismissing Zanzibar officials we were led ashore and locked up in hotel rooms. The teams began battling among themselves, and I was at the centre of a political farce which began to rock the stability of the Zanzibar Government. On the third day I requested to talk to my ambassador in Dar-es-Salaam, and as a result of our telephone conversation he despatched a young embassy attaché to come to my rescue.

Mr Melano arrived four hours later by private plane and proclaimed me a sound citizen of the Republic of Italy, destined to sail Arab dhows for reasons beyond human comprehension. So the troublesome thorn was plucked from their side, and the *Mir-El-Lah* left for Dar-es-Salaam.

Even in this busy harbour the *Mir-El-Lah* caused quite a stir, and a crowd of old timers, stevedores and sailors gathered round to ask questions. There is dhow traffic in both Zanzibar and Dar-es-Salaam, mostly by *jahazis* – coastal vessels, smaller cousins of my ocean-going dhow, which trade with Kenya and occasionally Somalia.

We sailed on south to Mafia Island and I entered its difficult lagoon with great caution; the sea and tides meet in this narrow passage, and tremendous whirlpools break with fury on the black volcanic rocks fringing the edges.

In Mafia I found more political problems and more bewildered policemen disbelieving the authority of our visas. I was ordered to return to Dar-es-Salaam to confirm the permission which had been granted for me to sail from there to Mafia! I objected strongly to this madness, but was told that if I did not return to Dar-es-Salaam superior officers there would believe I had bribed the Mafia officials.

I intended to ignore this order, but before sailing south I visited a small dhow-building yard near the ancient ruins on Mafia. I pushed my way through a very dark green forest whose roots and branches enveloped the remains of two- and three-storey Arab buildings. Flamboyant red petals cascaded along my path, forming a soft carpet and diffusing a powerful perfume. I imagined the settlement bustling with activity in its prosperous past, the dhows anchored in the lagoon near the shore of this ghost city inhabited now only by parrots, squirrels, lizards and snakes.

I sailed on south to the isle of Songo-Songo in the Rufiji delta, and only then did I turn northwards to Dar-es-Salaam and back to Kilifi, where my

Previous page Mirella had asked me to bring back some fish for supper. I brought a rock cod

Kimuyu caught, cooked and served fish often within minutes

clients disembarked, very happy with their adventure. I then began preparations for my journey to the Seychelles.

This was to be a very special dhow voyage. I had to learn how to use a sextant, and I started to pick up astronomical notions from books and friends. I drew up an Arab-style itinerary, a straight line from Kilifi to L'Aigle, the nearest island of the Amirantes Group, nine hundred miles away. It is hardly possible to miss Africa when sailing west from the Seychelles, but it is not at all difficult to miss the Seychelles sailing east from Africa. If I were to miss them, I would have much sea water ahead of me before reaching the nearest land.

I found myself whistling the French children's song '*Il-y-avait un p'tit navire*' while plotting not only a course to the Seychelles, but also emergency courses to Madagascar or the Comoro Islands, or back to Africa, or northeast to the Maldives or Ceylon. As a result of all this plotting I doubled my fuel reserve to a staggering twelve forty-four-gallon drums, enough for a five-thousand-mile trip. If my navigation was poor, I could always return to Africa and Kilifi. I also fitted out my rubber dinghy with a green canvas lateen sail cut from an old tent, and filled it with cans of water, fishing gear and emergency provisions. I felt better with that dinghy stashed on deck.

I soon discovered that using a nautical almanac was, for me, very difficult. I found out that to establish one's position one must first know where one is! That is, you must at least know you are in the Indian Ocean near the equator and somewhere between Kilifi and the Seychelles. In this way you have restricted the world to a square with sides of about five hundred miles. In other words you are pinpointing your exact position on your 'assumed' one. Luckily there are tables and sextant to help. What did emerge from all these efforts was that I acquired a deeper faith in natural phenomena. In the southern hemisphere my most useful constellation was the Southern Cross; it helped greatly, but not with the incredible precision of Polaris. To cut a long story short, I would not advise anybody to attempt to navigate as I did.

I felt that, if I could reach the Seychelles, Christopher Columbus could hardly have missed the Caribbean. This new knowledge of mine certainly did tarnish the image I had of our great seafarers. I acquired a compass and some elementary books on navigation with sentences beginning: 'Even a child of six could steer your boat to the Galapagos,' or 'Your blind grandmother could get a fix on the lower lip of the moon by following these instructions.' The prize example was *The Kindergarten for Celestial Navigation*, an American book written so simply that apparently even a pet chimpanzee could learn how to navigate!

I loaded all my provisions ready to sail: two live goats (male and female), rabbits, chickens, seeds and a miniature vegetable garden. I even had a coconut which had sprouted in a plastic bucket full of water. When in London I always believed that if I carried an umbrella it would not rain; now I was prepared for any number of shipwrecks – even my Mark III rubber dinghy had its own tender, a Mark I.

Two of my friends, Bob Zagury and Barry Allen, sailed with me, and the objective of our Seychelles trip was to attract and observe big sharks underwater. Our departure date had long passed by: frankly, it was perhaps delayed by fear. I felt like a child trying to pluck up courage to dive from a high board into a swimming-pool.

I had entered a fishing competition sponsored by British Airways; the first prize was three return tickets from Nairobi to the Seychelles. I had told everybody I would win so that Mirella, Marina and Amina could join me in Mahé, the largest of the Seychelles islands, by courtesy of British Airways.

On the day before the competition the *muallimu* (an Islamic priest) slaughtered a goat and sprinkled its blood on the deck of my brand-new

fishing boat *Next Year*, burned incense and intoned words from the Koran.
Simba, who had been persuaded to come to the Seychelles with us, insisted
that another goat be sacrificed on the dhow. I am by nature superstitious,
probably because of the Neapolitan blood running through my veins, and it
was not difficult to accept other people's superstitions and make them my
own. I knew very well that to win a fishing competition with sixty-five boats
competing would be far more difficult than reaching the Seychelles by
dhow, so I decided to out-do superstition completely by telling everyone I
would win. I even bought my own boat in a sweepstake, and hoping to
break the long tradition that whoever buys his own boat in this way never
wins the competition.

To catch a big fish one is supposed to use an old rod and a rusty hook, to
let the bait trail unguarded, go to the loo and read; no one ready and keen
ever catches one. I sat ready and keen, wearing polaroid glasses, and gloves,
and trailing a magnificent freshly caught mullet. Madeka steered the boat
wherever he fancied. Everyone else headed north; Madeka and I went south.
They all went to the best spots near Watamu. Madeka kept close to the reef
of Takaungu. The fishing had been bad for weeks; I had from 6 a.m. till
1 p.m. to win. We saw nothing, not one dorsal fin, not even a porpoise
leaping out of the water; it was like shooting hundreds of rounds into a blue
summer sky, hoping to hit a duck.

At noon, with one hour to go, we turned for home. We were about a mile
from shore and the only boat in sight was two miles to the north. Suddenly I
saw a splash. My muscles tightened as if hit by an electric shock. The mullet
I trawled disappeared in a twirl of foam, the reel screamed. One hundred
yards of line went out, then two hundred, and three. A black marlin rose out
of the water and leaped once in a perfect semi-circle. No words were uttered
as Madeka adjusted his course a little. I felt cool, calm and collected,
although I knew my eighty-pound test-line was worn, frayed and barby.

Suddenly the reel screamed again and at once my fish was on his tail
running on the surface like a tightrope walker. He shook his massive head,
then plunged back into the water and sounded. I played the line with my
thumb – it was all I could do now. I willed the fish to stay on. I told him how
important it was for me and my family. He was deep down now, rolling and
twisting; I could feel the line stretching out. I knew how easily it could snap.
Then I thought of sharks, for mutilation would disqualify the fish. I glanced
at Madeka, who looked down at me with his big flashy smile. Ben, my
fisherman friend, and Barry Allen were behind me and I turned to them and
said, 'Now. Have the gaff ready.'

Overleaf Myself and Mirella on the deck of the *Mir-El-Lah* at Zanzibar

'*Hapana*,' said Ben. ('No.')

'You sure, Ben? It's big.'

'*Hapana* – no gaff,' repeated Ben in Swahili. 'I'm sure. I'll take him with my hands. I'm stronger than he is.'

I turned, placing my feet on the transom, and started reeling in, pumping the fish up. Madeka kept the boat in line with the tip of the rod. Ben saw the fish first and moved to the transom; it came up easily, doing what I asked. He was tired. I reeled it in smoothly and firmly; it was now almost under the boat, a foot maybe from the surface. Ben looked at me. I nodded. Barry held the *rungu* (club), Madeka kept the engine in gear – forward, slow. The fish followed, waving its tail in the churning wake. Ben bent down slowly and stretched out his powerful arms until he had the fish by its bill. The muscles in his chest expanded; he moved steadily and powerfully. He knew that the fish was doomed. When the head appeared well out of the water, Barry struck with the club while Ben eased the fish over the transom into the boat.

Madeka came down from the flying bridge to touch the fish and I shook his hand, still not believing our success. 'Let's get home quickly,' I said. The boat near us had been circling all the time out of the way and was now heading back. I kept thinking there could be a bigger bill-fish, or maybe two smaller ones caught by one of those sixty-five boats. I hoisted the blue flag to signal I had a marlin on board and noticed a similar flag on another boat. I prayed it would not be bigger. It wasn't. Mine was just under two hundred pounds, the other just over a hundred.

I phoned Mirella in Naivasha as soon as possible. In reply to her question had I won the competition I answered, 'Yes, of course I did.' I told her to go to the British Airways office in Nairobi to collect the three tickets. I don't think she believed my story. She said she would take her cheque-book, just in case.

18. The Seychelles

A week later when we sailed for the Amirantes Islands, part of the
Seychelles group, the moon was almost full, and while the lights of
Mombasa faded I watched the *Mir-El-Lah*'s silvery wake. The sea was
calm, there was no wind; thanks to our engine we made good headway.

Every morning we pointed into the rising sun, and at night I was
comforted to see the Southern Cross over our starboard side. Bob studied
celestial navigation, while Barry became the referee in the numerous
disputes over our exact position. We picked up the BBC on the radio, for
Bob needed Greenwich Mean Time to fix it; time and again my estimated
position coincided with Bob's, but he believed it was just luck. I distrusted
his 'instant' seamanship. Barry disbelieved both of us. Madeka and Kimuyu
trusted us implicitly; and Simba, a true Bajun sailor, thought that seeing was
believing and spent most of his time at the bows on the look-out for the
island we were hoping to reach, Ramire (The Eagle).

We met with sperm whales and flying fish; we ate, we slept, we read. And
on the fourth night Simba, peering into the blackness, pointed ahead and
said, 'Land.' The Amirantes are flat coral islands surrounded by reefs with
coconut palms and casuarina trees. I swept the horizon with my glasses and
picked up the slight relief of a low island. If it was Ramire, our navigation,
celestial or magic, would have been perfect. I woke everybody up.

'Land,' I said.

'Ramire?' asked Bob.

'Could be,' I replied.

The air seemed to glow, with a dark purple halo outlining the island as if a
pencil had traced round its contour. The sun rose quickly behind palm trees
that looked like green flowers in a bucket. By seven o'clock we could clearly
see the sand and corals on the seabed thirty feet below. There were fish
everywhere, and Kimuyu let out a line. The feather jig had hardly hit the
water when the huge reel shrieked madly; Madeka slammed the gear into
neutral, while Barry steered hard to starboard. Half the line was already
gone, five hundred yards of Dacron, the rod bent double.

Such a powerful fish in such shallow water did not seem to make sense; at the speed it was going it could not be a shark, and the only fish I could think of was a very large *mahoo*. After a long fight I brought it to gaff and had a hard struggle to hoist it on deck – an eighty-pound dog-toothed tunny, a fish I had never caught before, and a tremendous fighter.

We dodged the reefs and approached the lee shore, where a small fishing schooner was anchored with three men standing by the gunwale.

'*Bonjour*,' I cried. '*Où sommes-nous?* Ramire?'

'*Oui, oui,* Ramire!' they shouted back.

'How about that?' I said, turning to Bob.

The men I had been shouting to were an amazing combination of colour and blood. One had a yellowish-brown skin with thick furry hair, his nose aquiline, his eyes the bluest blue; he could have been twenty or fifty. Another was the twin brother of Vincent Van Gogh; the third was a black man with pink lips and ears. As our anchor went down, theirs came up and they set their sails against the orange ball of the rising sun.

We swam ashore to a beach littered with shells, and walked towards a luminous green forest of coconut palms and dense wet undergrowth. Hundreds of large black-and-yellow spiders had woven their webs between the tree trunks and we slashed them away with sticks; it was impossible to avoid all the webs, and very unpleasant when we couldn't. The island appeared to be uninhabited. Wild chickens flew ahead of us and a pig dashed through the thicket. We retrieved our shotgun from the dhow and a few hours later had lunch on the beach: *coq au vin à la Bajun*, so tough that we used pliers to tear the meat apart.

I discovered an abandoned village, several wooden houses on stilts with beds and rotten mattresses. There was a shed with a longboat standing on wooden blocks; the timber was brittle, dry and completely rotten. In one of the huts I found old papers and a book half eaten by rats and worms. On its cover was a coat of arms with a turtle, a king's coconut in the middle, an island on the left and a schooner on the right. Underneath was an inscription: *Finis coronat opus* – 'the end crowns the work'. The first words I could make out were '. . . delectable but sometimes inscrutable colony . . .'. On opening it I discovered it was about the Seychelles.

Chapter 1 began, 'The Arabs . . .', which immediately excited me. I read that Arab manuscripts dating back to AD 810, mentioned one Al Masoudi who had visited Madagascar and stopped over in a group of islands 'beyond the Maldives'. An Arab chart mentioned the island of the Rukh and commented: 'The Rukh was described by Marco Polo as a gigantic eagle with a wingspan of a hundred and fifty feet which carried off and devoured elephants. The Great Khan, anxious to obtain one, sent an envoy who returned with a quill from the fabulous bird. Ibn Battuta, a writer-traveller, said he saw a Rukh when he visited the East African coast and the Maldives in the fourteenth century.'

The book described many famous visitors to the islands. Stanley, the explorer, spent a month in a cottage named after Dr Livingstone. General Gordon was there in 1881; he wrote an essay seeking to prove that Praslin Island was the site of the Garden of Eden and the Coco de Mer was the forbidden fruit. Once, when dining with a Mr Estridge, the latter remarked that Eve could hardly have bitten into a coconut as the husk is some four inches thick. 'I never thought of that,' said General Gordon.

A gunshot brought me back to reality: Bob was advancing holding a cockerel with a long tail and thick yellow spurs, razor sharp. A chick of the Rukh, I thought, fingering his claws.

I suggested we return to the dhow for a shark-hunting dive. Kimuyu had been fishing and the decks were strewn with silvery bodies, so I insisted that no more fish be caught and dried.

When we were ready to dive I thought of the film *Jaws*, which I had seen in Mombasa a week earlier. Perhaps I have a shark *djinn*, as I have been diving for so many years in sharky waters, but I had never yet seen a large one. When I dive, cartwheeling into new waters, I feel like a fly cast into a pond with a monster waiting nearby to pounce.

Here in Ramire the water was clear as champagne and Madeka had no difficulty in following us, swimming along pushing the dinghy and observing us from the surface. There were many small underwater canyons, with large brain corals surrounded by bushes of stag corals with russet antlers. Hundreds of large red snappers, greatly agitated by our visit, rushed in and out of deep crevasses. Barry harpooned a fish and we waited as the green blood diffused into the water, the best way to attract sharks. A few small ones came, but no monsters. Big sharks are very shy and dislike the noise and bubbles of aqualungs.

On our way back to the dhow I trailed a fishing hand-line from the dinghy. A tremendous jolt pulled my hand and the coil unwound, but the fish stopped fighting very soon. I guessed correctly that it was a barracuda. When we saw it behind the dinghy gliding gently in the current we realised we had a problem: it was longer than the dinghy, the biggest barracuda I had ever seen, six to seven feet long. Bob solved the problem by sliding gently into the water and shooting a harpoon behind the fish's gills.

After a few days in this timelessly beautiful place we sailed to Mahé (the largest of the Seychelles islands). I had heard that in its capital, Port Victoria, the authorities were very finicky over regulations, so I promptly hoisted a yellow flag to indicate that we were ready for inspection. After we had passed it we moved to the inter-islands schooners' pier where I saw three finely engraved bronze cannons chained to a gate; they had been left there by an American yacht's crew who had found them somewhere near the Amirantes. These islands are famed for sunken treasure.

A telegram for Simba informed him that one of his seventeen children was very ill, and to obtain an exit permit we were told to see a Mr Marimba, head of immigration. I imagined that anyone with such a melodious name could not be anything but helpful; but unfortunately Mr Marimba proved to be a bitter bureaucrat who had mislaid his sense of humour in a thick forest of red tape. We waited five days to get permission before Simba could return to Kenya, his homeland.

The officials did not like the look of us and our 'galleon'; in their minds we were hippies and 'corsairs'. We were never allowed into the yacht basin, and we were boarded, disturbed and searched by the police almost every day.

As soon as possible we left Mahé for Bird Island, a low coral islet located at the northern edge of the Seychelles' coral plateau, famous for its seabirds. Here there is an almost vertical drop of thousands of feet into the deep. Surely here we would meet the monsters we were looking for. At the beginning of our first dive we were nervous and kept looking from left to right as if we were watching tennis at Wimbledon. We had decided to swim in a rotating circle so that together we would have 360° of vision all the time. We placed ourselves some forty feet apart, ready to converge back to back under the rubber dinghy if necessary.

In the sparkling clear water my friends made an impressive sight, suspended almost motionless with speargun in one hand and fanning the water gently with the other in order to remain upright in the current. Like *toreros* of the sea, waiting in the arena for our adversary to attack.

On our right hung the vertical cliff of Bird Island's coral reef; down below to our left the bluest blue I shall ever see. We were sixty feet down, and along the cliff some huge groupers and other massive fish watched us with great curiosity. We were big fish ourselves, six feet long, one-hundred-and-fifty-pounders; black fish with stinging barbs. There were no sharks.

We decided to attract them with food; on our return to the dhow I prepared five hooks dangling from a mile-long Japanese line. Each hook was tied to a six-foot chain leading to a buoy floating on the surface. The main line was attached to the cliff by one end, by the other to a forty-four-gallon drum floating half a mile off-shore. To the drum I tied one hundred feet of eight-millimetre chain with one of the dhow's anchors at the end. Each hook was baited with ten pounds of fish speared on the spot.

I believed that the sharks would strike only at night, but I was wrong. After about an hour we decided to patrol the line on the surface and found that all five hooks had already been swallowed by small sharks about five feet long. They seemed calm and resigned, like dogs on a leash. The sun was setting, and I did not wish to remain any longer in the water, so we left them. It was the first time ever I had used hundred-pound sharks as live bait.

Early next morning we returned to see a strange, awesome spectacle. The five buoys were massed round the drum, which was listing heavily. I swam down close to the cliff to investigate this jam and found that the line had been wrenched off the coral and that the chains were all knotted up in a hopeless tangle. The anchor had hooked onto a rock protruding from the cliff and I had to dive down to free it. I found myself facing the head of one of the sharks used as bait: the white vitreous eyes popped out as if the fish had been strangled before being eaten.

Only one hook remained – the others had disappeared, torn from their chains. Only monster sharks could be responsible for this, I thought, nervously looking at my legs as I followed the anchor chain down in order to disengage the anchor. My precious Sekoyama line and the five leaders with their chains were so tangled that we had to cut them up into pieces.

We now knew the monsters were there and we were determined to catch, or at least catch sight of, them. We cut up two hundred pounds of fish and filled a sack with the bloody meat. We dangled the sack fifty feet under the dinghy and dived in, hovering over the sack which trailed a cloud of greenish blood as it drifted with the current. If a monster picked up the scent he would follow the current to the sack. We eventually had hundreds of small sharks circling round the sack, tearing it open. When morsels of fish started to float all around us we had to retreat to the dinghy: a bite from a five-foot shark can sever an arm or take a good chunk out of a human body. The beasts were in a frenzy and there were too many of them for safety; even standing back to back we could not prod them away quickly enough.

Before surfacing I injected one of the largest with a CO_2 cartridge which shoots bubbles into the bloodstream, causing an embolism. The shark spiralled up to the surface, seemingly dead, but after a while it regained its senses and dived down to continue its lunch. From the dinghy we could see hundreds of them fighting over each piece of meat, tearing the sack greedily and swallowing the pieces. But where were the monsters?

A local fisherman told us that in a place called Anse Boudin near Praslin Island there is a channel so thick with sharks that by jumping from back to back you can cross without getting your feet wet! I could not resist this, so we sailed to Anse Boudin to see for ourselves. Other fishermen confirmed that twenty-foot tiger and hammerhead sharks had been caught there; one went on to say that in the last few years 'German tourists had eaten them all'.

When we told the fishermen that we proposed to dive at night they said that there was enough takamaka wood in the islands to make coffins for our souls, for our bodies would never surface again. The 'big black beasts' would cut us in two before we could even shine our torches on them.

The beach at Grande Anse is covered with broken shells. The longboats of the fishermen are pulled up under the palms. In the old wooden houses on stilts the women work and raise their children, while on the beach below the men prepare their fishing gear and build other boats. Five carpenters were at work just opposite the *Mir-El-Lah* – I had tied her to the palms, for owing to her shallow draught it was often possible to beach her on the shore. In this way I could smell the cooking-fires, hear the people talk and converse with them when I wanted to; I could lend and borrow, invite and be invited by these people of the sea.

That night they all came to see the last of us. I caught one of them crossing himself when we slid down into the black water of the channel and I took it as a good omen. We flashed our torches into the water, making sure that each one of us would light up the feet of the diver in front. The shark I fear the most is the one I don't see, the one that steals up behind to cut me in half before I know he is there.

The beams of our torches startled many fish, lobsters and shellfish that night, but they never shone on the beady eyes of a monster or on his rows of triangular teeth. We stood back to back forty feet down, moving just enough to keep floating and searching the depths with our torches until they ran out of power. Then we surfaced, to see several longboats full of curious spectators surrounding Madeka and Kimuyu in the dinghy and shaking their heads in disbelief.

'German tourists *have* eaten them all,' I told them, removing my flippers.

In three months of diving we never saw a shark larger than five feet. Barry and Bob had to return home and I remained there alone until Mirella, Marina and Amina arrived. I met them at Victoria, the capital of Mahé, and we sailed off to La Digue, where we dived for shells and Amina managed to find several rare cowries on the seabed. 'Look, look, Daddy, look what I've found,' she would shout excitedly, swimming towards me like a Labrador retrieving a duck. We rode astride the giant turtles of Bird Island and fed the fairy terns. We dug oysters from the rocks and ate them in the sea, and drank coconut milk. At night we listened to the surf and slept beneath the palms.

The south-eastern monsoon had begun to push heavy clouds northwards and we were hit by thunderstorms and rain squalls. The canvas roof over the poop gathered enormous quantities of water. In the cabins, radios, cassettes, books, charts, instruments, fishing gear, the lot were wet, rusty or mouldy. The sun by itself was not enough to dry up the persistent humidity. The dhow badly needed a wooden roof.

One night while at anchor at Anse Boudin I dangled a baited hook in the water from my largest rod. A sudden storm rose, wind and rain lashed at us. We heard the unexpected scream of the reel. Amina and Marina rushed for it, Mirella flashed a torch, and I tightened the 'drag'. The *Mir-El-Lah* shifted on her anchor as if a monster had decided to tow her out to sea. The children watched excitedly. How long would the line hold out? It was a weird sensation being towed at night on a fifty-ton vessel by a mysterious underwater creature. Then suddenly the rod sprang up and the line went slack. I reeled it in: the hook was gone. 'It was the *Shaitani* [the devil],' Kimuyu said, flashing his eyes and summing up our thoughts.

The next morning half a dozen policemen from the coastguard cutter came aboard with a search warrant. They claimed we had drugs and arms hidden. An arrogant uniformed officer began questioning Marina, who was only fourteen years old. He asked whether her father smoked 'strange-smelling cigarettes'. Marina looked at him and replied: 'If you mean does Daddy smoke pot, the answer is no.'

The same man produced a .22 calibre Fiocchi cartridge and asked if it were mine. I had given it to an owl bounty hunter on La Digue: the owls there are accounted vermin, as they kill the birds. I took the bullet from him and dropped it overboard as if by mistake.

'I'm terribly sorry,' I said. 'I've lost your evidence.'

After a long painstaking search without results the man left, but that night I buried my shotgun and .22 pistol wrapped in greased rags and tinfoil on the island of Aride.

When my family went to the airport to fly home they were officially declared *persona non grata* on the grounds that they had not received a booster cholera injection on arrival. It was futile to retort that no one had enforced this regulation, or that there had been no one at the airport to administer the jab. Their 'deportation' was a parting gift for the 'hippies of the dhow', the new 'corsairs' of the *Mir-El-Lah*.

Overleaf Amina with a giant turtle in the Seychelles. It was 'love at low tide'

19. The Outer Islands

At La Digue a seventy-foot schooner, *La Belle Vue*, was anchored next to us. The owner, Monsieur Grégoire, told me he needed a mate to help Captain Alphonse sail her to the outer islands with a British medical expedition. They were to collect mosquitoes on Providence Island, Farquhar, Astove, Cosmoledo Assumption and Aldabra, a voyage of two thousand miles. I doubt if M. Grégoire would have offered me the job had he been aware of my navigational capabilities, but he insisted on calling me 'Captain' and offered me an attractive salary.

Within twenty-four hours the Government of the Seychelles validated my Panamanian ticket for the job in question and I was, so to speak, incorporated in the Seychelles Navy. The Customs people immediately ceased harassing me: I had become 'respectable', no longer a 'corsair'. During my absence Madeka and Kimuyu would remain in the *Mir-El-Lah* at La Digue.

The medical expedition consisted of two English doctors and four Seychellois assistants. The crew of *La Belle Vue* was from La Digue. We loaded a mixed cargo for Providence and Farquhar islands. I was very excited to be embarking on a scientific sea voyage full of romantic undertones. Celestial navigation or not, there was no doubt in my mind that I would bring the schooner home, by magic or by instinct if necessary.

We set sail for Providence in good weather; Captain Alphonse, the skipper, was asleep and I took *La Belle Vue* out of Mahé. Her two masts were each sixty feet high; I was determined to climb them once out at sea.

The doctors seemed to be happy at my presence and commented frequently on my good seamanship and obvious experience. I, of course, could only agree with them as modestly as possible! Our course took us between Mahé and Silhouette, the highest island in the group. As we lost sight of the islands I marked our position on the chart, wondering when we would next sight land.

Captain Alphonse then told me cheerfully about the two Savy brothers who ran into a gale crossing from Mahé to Bird Island to collect seabirds' eggs. They had drifted fourteen hundred miles to Arabia, four of the crew

218

died, and a fifth was whisked off into the desert by Bedus. The Savy brothers themselves managed to reach Muscat by camel and returned to the Seychelles via Bombay a year later.

Having watched me stow away my diving gear, the Captain tried to interest me in wrecks. The French frigate *L'Heureuse*, he told me, wrecked off Providence Island in 1793 with treasure on board. He knew the marks of the wreck, and he reeled off a long list of others. After looking furtively behind him he whispered: 'You and I, we shall return in your dhow.'

This was the second proposition I had received to search for treasure. A well-known merchant of Mahé had told me the story of the Chinaman Lin Fung To who, heavily in debt, had accepted the job of guardian of the island of La Poule, one of the Amirantes. After six months of solitude he dug up the graves in the local cemetery and found gold fillings in the teeth of several skulls. On his return to Mahé he made a small ingot from the gold and sold it to the local jeweller. Everybody believed that Ling Fung To had found hidden treasure, and many 'friends' bought him drinks to loosen his tongue. In a few months the Chinaman became an alcoholic and one night, going home drunk, was drowned in a ditch in the town of Victoria. There were rumours that he had left a will with a map of the location of his treasure.

'But he merely found gold fillings in some skulls,' I pointed out to the merchant.

'That is what everybody believes,' he said, lowering his voice. 'But I have bought his will and the map.'

We arrived safely in Providence, and as soon as we were anchored the crew began fishing. They were professionals and turned the schooner into a production line. One baited the hook, another threw it into the sea, a third held his hand high to strike the fish. Another man hoisted and despatched it before it even touched the deck, and the last cleaned and salted it away.

In the role of an assistant I followed the doctors ashore and watched them sucking mosquitoes through a long glass pipe into a jar. They sucked mosquitoes from the walls of houses and from our own bodies. They were concerned with philariasis, for the mosquitoes of these islands were not malaria carriers.

A tall woman with flowing red hair, green eyes and a well-displayed bosom 'covered' by a lacy blouse came forward to greet me. '*Mon capitain,*' she said, '*bienvenu à Providence.*' I was flattered, and bent to kiss her hand. She was Yvonne, wife of the Superintendent of Providence Island, a graceful, sexy, happy soul who radiated joy wherever she went. She told me that she had prepared a lobster curry for us and that her toddy was the best in all the island: '*Vous allez voir, Monsieur le capitain, vous allez voir.*'

She was obviously the Queen of Providence, reigning from a large house on stilts over several *laboureurs*, many chickens and ducks, a few dogs and pigs, half a dozen cats, five of her children and five thousand palm trees.

The island belonged to BIOT, British Indian Ocean Territory, a little-known state which includes a few islands scattered over thousands of miles. In the evening I followed Yvonne to lower the BIOT – British flag from its staff. While she was doing this she told me she had heard that day on her radio that the Americans had lost the war in Vietnam. I had completely forgotten the world.

That night in front of a bonfire Yvonne danced the *sega* (a cross between 'La Java' and a Haitian *merengue* which comes from Mauritius); with the two British doctors and a *Capitain de marine italien* in the audience Yvonne put all the fire she had in her veins into it.

In the morning before leaving I kissed her hand again. I regretted I did not have a wide-brimmed hat with feathers and a cape to complete this graceful gesture for Yvonne of Providence.

Monsieur Grégoire had promised a case of beer to the first man to sight Farquhar Island. I climbed to the top of the mast where I surveyed the horizon and, having timed our probable arrival on the chart, suddenly shouted 'Land!'

No one could see it; certainly not me. Rufus the cabin boy climbed to the top of the other mast and only after an hour did he sight land. I shared the case of beer with him and gave my six bottles to the crew. They were very impressed with my eyesight.

At Farquhar Island we unloaded the rest of our cargo – tinned food, two outboard engines, spare parts and fishing gear. Rufus told me that the Superintendent there would turn a blind eye if we wanted to spear a turtle or two to eat, so we prepared our whaler and, with Joseph the lancer, Rufus and Le Breton, we set out for the inner lagoon, a lake with a maze of coral formations within the ocean. We often had to push the whaler in the shallow water. All the time Joseph stood on the bow, brandishing his harpoon and scanning the flats. Eventually we sighted something too big to be a turtle, splashing about half a mile away. It was a tiger shark thrashing about on its belly and pectorals like a pig enjoying a mud bath. We saw only a few turtles and Joseph missed one, the only chance we had to vary our fish diet; turtle meat is white and tastes like veal, and makes a welcome change in places where one eats fish all the time.

That night the sky was clear and Captain Alphonse showed us how to find the most important constellations. This six-foot, two-hundred-pound man talked of the stars as if they were his friends and he would fix our position at the 'civil hour' by plotting a handful of them in the early morning or at dusk when the horizon was still visible and they are either fading away or just appearing.

We sailed to Astove atoll, a ring of coral containing a shallow, almost dry lagoon. An American had leased it for many years, but after his death it was managed by a lonely Englishman who did not stop talking from the moment we arrived. On the eastern coast of Astove the reef drops vertically to the bottom of the ocean. We could not anchor there with an inshore wind, so we left the schooner to drift out to sea with Joseph the lancer in charge. He could sail slowly up and down the shore with the auxiliary engine.

I dived with Rufus into the depths and found that the reef was shallower on the western side. I fell on an old anchor embedded in coral in thirty feet of water, and two old cannons encrusted with coral and velvety seaweed. This was probably the wreck of the *Dom Royal*, a seventeenth-century galleon, and we decided to try to hoist the anchor, which we needed for our schooner. Ten men, helped by the engine of *La Belle Vue*, could not budge it an inch. I wanted to try my luck with the cannons, but the wind was shifting and Captain Alphonse wanted to leave the *Dom Royal* alone and set sail immediately for Aldabra.

The south-eastern monsoon blew us at eight knots towards the atoll of Cosmoledo, which we sadly bypassed. Apparently the same mosquitoes existed there as on Aldabra. When we sighted land I again climbed to the top of the mast to enjoy the view with the birds. Flocks of boobies the size of small geese circled the schooner to welcome us. From my perch I could see the whole of the atoll, which was the size of an international airport, its ring of land dotted with palms and casuarina trees and long white spits of sand jutting into the sea.

I clutched the top of the mast as the boobies flew inches from my face and looked at me with their curious reddish-brown eyes. They tried to land on the steel cable connecting the two masts; with their outstretched webbed feet they endeavoured to grab the wire – obviously a difficult exercise. A few succeeded but many missed and lost their back feathers, cartwheeling or somersaulting forward, squawking like the Furies. They tried over and over again until one by one they managed to land. Once they were on the cable they had to use all the equilibrium they possessed to stay on, jerking like puppets on a string. When all the front-row seats were taken a few

latecomers tried to land on my head. This was the moment when I decided
that I had seen enough of Cosmoledo from the air.

We reached Aldabra late in the afternoon. The atoll, seven miles long and
four wide, is leased to the Royal Society of London and is inhabited by a
dozen scientists and their retinue of Seychellois. A nature reserve, Aldabra
is to the Indian Ocean what the Galapagos Islands are to the Pacific. To land
we lowered the whaler, waiting for the right moment to cross the reef, which
Rufus signalled by shouting '*Veille l'embellie*' ('Wait the good moment') in
Seychellois. The whaler then slid over the reef, riding the crest of the waves
and kept in line by the oars.

The first scientist I met on the beach, Mr Swingland, told me that there
are more than one hundred and fifty thousand giant tortoise still living on
the atoll. The smallest are the size of a cake of soap, the largest the size of a
baby's pram. He kept some of them in paddocks for his studies. At night
their mating calls echoed off the reefs. As Swingland took me over this last
virtually undisturbed paradise he told me that the British and the United
States air forces had both surveyed the island with a view to turning it into
a military base.

The weather was deteriorating, and Captain Alphonse began fretting, so
we headed north-east for Mahé, seven hundred miles away. The south-
eastern wind would be in our favour so long as the six-foot shallow draught
of *La Belle Vue* did not set us too much out of course towards the African
coast. We had run out of fuel and would be sailing all the way. I realised then
that we could never have reached the Seychelles with only the *Mir-El-
Lah*'s lateen rig.

I was afraid we might drift south and lose our way through the
Almirantes, or run aground on the almost invisible reef of The Pearls. In
five days, I estimated, we could easily drift a hundred miles to the south.
Suddenly we heard a thundering cracking noise: the boom had split. With
all hands we lowered the mainsail while Captain Alphonse eased the
schooner into the wind, and in a few hours we had repaired the damage and
hoisted the sail again.

We were sleeping badly in coffin-like berths; rivulets of water, swept in by
the wind or seeping through the roof, soaked our mattresses and clothes. It
was cold, and the clouds never allowed Captain Alphonse to fix our position.
The schooner was sailing on a close reach, constantly leaning to port. The
sea kept her decks awash all the time and there was nowhere we could go
when we were off duty other than to our foul-smelling box-like cabins.

On the fifth day, when I asked the Captain where we were, he shrugged and said that Mahé was ahead and the Amirantes to starboard. On the sixth day I made myself a nest by the bowsprit with the storm jibs and gazed north, hoping to sight land. The doctors summoned me to their cabin and asked when we would arrive and I told them optimistically 'within twenty-four hours'. The next day at noon Joseph, the bos'n, climbed up the mast but saw no land. By the evening I had not seen even a single bird and I was gloomy. Despite drizzling rain I took up my position forward, and just before midnight, after drying the lenses of my binoculars, I swept the horizon. I saw a glow dead ahead. Was it a light, or a star? I called Rufus, trusting his sharp eyesight better than mine. 'It is the light from the American tracking station on Mahé,' he announced gleefully.

Within twenty-four hours I was on board the *Mir-El-Lah*. In my bed I found a charming girl, one of Madeka's conquests from La Digue. When I was last there I had picked up a mynah bird with a broken wing and had nursed it back to health, baptising it 'Monsieur La Digue'. I found his remains lying on the bottom of his cage. Kimuyu told me that the bird would not eat or drink. When I asked if they had given him anything to eat or drink his reply was a laconic 'No, bwana, so sorry, bwana.'

It was time to return to Kenya. Before leaving I went to Praslin Island to find more cowrie shells for my collection. During my first dive I kicked a long-spiked sea urchin with such force that dozens of barbs sank deep into my right foot. I had to cut off my flipper to remove them. Twenty-four hours later my foot was the size of a melon and very painful, and the next morning we had to sail for Kenya. I stuffed myself full of antibiotics and sleeping-pills at night and, placing my mattress on deck, guided my two archers from Machakos at the wheel. But I did have to give them a hand to hoist the lateen – not easy with my pulsating swollen foot.

I was comforted by the fact that by sailing westwards we could not miss Africa. I steered towards the setting sun, and at night the Southern Cross on the left led me on. The weather improved, the sky cleared, and the wind remained fair and steady. Our sail filled and the *Mir-El-Lah* settled gently to port, making good speed.

On the morning of the fifth day I decided to try out my call-buoy radio on 2182, the emergency frequency; I had never used it before. 'Dhow *Mir-El-Lah*, dhow *Mir-El-Lah*,' I repeated, 'calling Mombasa, calling Mombasa.' I was really surprised when I heard a friendly voice answering 'Mombasa radio, Mombasa radio, I read you loud and clear.' Indeed I was so taken aback that I was at a loss for words; I felt as if I had called to God and He had answered. I said: 'I am happy you read me loud and clear, I am so very happy, and thank you very much. Out.'

This foolish conversation proved, however, that I was approximately fifty miles off the Kenyan coast, the range of my small emergency radio.

At noon we sighted land but, although we closed in, I could not tell exactly where we were. I almost had to ram the dark continent before realising that I was near Watamu and Kilifi. This one-thousand-mile crossing, together with the one from Sirri to Dubai with the *shamal*, had been the best of my nautical career.

At five in the afternoon we dropped anchor below my house. I knew that Ali Sururu, the dhow harbourmaster at Mombasa, would not mind my skipping his control; he knew that I only carried a cargo of dreams.

When I stepped ashore my swollen foot made me trip on a branch across the path leading to my home and I grabbed hold of a rotten rail on which a ten-foot pole was leaning; the pole came crashing down on my head. At the end of it was a six-inch rusty nail which split open my forehead. I thought my last moment had come. I began bleeding profusely. When Kimuyu came to help me to my feet he shouted, '*Mungu, Bwana nakufa!*' ('God, Bwana is dead!')

My head healed quite quickly, I suppose, but it was three months before I could walk properly again.

20. Return to Aldabra and Cosmoledo

At this time I received an interesting offer which would have put the *Mir-El-Lah* to very good use. There was a surplus of white rhinos in Umfolozi National Park in South Africa which had to be moved. I flew down and took part in the capture of several young animals. We fired darts at them from a helicopter whose doors had been removed; swooping down on them, we chased them out of the bush into the open, flying often below tree-top level, a scary operation. I obtained twelve rhino calves from the South Africa park which were to be embarked in the *Mir-El-Lah* in Beira, Mozambique. I would sail them to Mombasa where the Kenya officials would accept them as a personal gift, thus avoiding otherwise insurmountable political problems.

The young rhinos were already in their *bomas*, and all the paperwork had been completed, when the political situation in Mozambique erupted. The rhinos were not allowed to travel by road to Beira, and I could not pick them up in Durban as the trip would be too long and the risks too high. So my Noah's Ark project went on the rocks. This was particularly unfortunate as the last white rhinos left in Kenya were soon to die in the Meru National Park.

I had left the *Mir-El-Lah* for several months below my house in the creek at Kilifi. When I returned from South Africa she had suffered from heat and humidity: barnacles and green algae had covered her hull below the waterline. Birds had nested inside the cabins and covered the planks with white droppings. The metal had rusted, brass had tarnished, and I could see the daylight through the decks. For a month Kimuyu, Madeka and I rubbed linseed oil into her timbers; we scraped and polished inside, outside and underneath. The *Mir-El-Lah* had aged, nails fell off her ribs like rotten teeth, water trickled in and many spars needed replacements. We did our best to show her that we still loved her. I hoped she would understand and forgive me for having neglected her through the long and abnormally wet rainy season.

I was mentally preparing the crossing from Mombasa to Cape Town and to Rio de Janeiro which would require a more responsible handling of the vessel and more accurate navigation than I had achieved so far. The *Mir-El-*

Overleaf Amina facing the Indian Ocean from Cosmoledo atoll.
Far beyond her gaze lies the South Pole

Lah needed ten tons of ballast and a mizzen to suit the square rig; a long bowsprit would allow me the use of three jibs. Colin Mudie, the well-known boat designer from Lymington in Hampshire, had worked out a new 'brigantine' rigging for my dhow (*see* p. 189). Optimistically I decided to carry out these important modifications myself. I bought a secondhand telegraph pole in Mombasa and transported it forty miles to Kilifi strapped to the roof-rack of my station wagon – a hair-raising experience. With the help of two cabinet-makers I fitted the twenty-two-foot-long bowsprit to the *Mir-El-Lah*. She suddenly reminded me of Pinocchio. Two days after completing this desecration a gun-boat of the Kenya Navy swept into the creek past her. The bowsprit did not survive the pitching and rolling caused by the PT boat – it came crashing down into the water where it bobbed pathetically, held by stays. I felt relieved: it could have happened in a storm in mid-ocean. Any further modification could now wait until I reached Cape Town with a lateen rig. A qualified boat-builder would do the transformations.

By early January I was ready to set sail again for Aldabra, a return to Paradise. From there I intended to go on to Cosmoledo, Astove and Assumption, islands on the northern fringe of the South Indian Ocean cyclonic belt. Dar-es-Salaam, where I could seek shelter if the weather deteriorated, was four hundred miles to the east.

My crew consisted of Mirella and Amina, Bob Zagury and Tuesday, a New York model, and of course Kimuyu and Madeka. We hired Juma to help them. In Mombasa we picked up the mail bag for the Royal Society station in Aldabra and set off cheerfully despite the *Mir-El-Lah*'s sulking. Her gear box wept oily tears, and a sparky alternator brought back memories of our Arabian Gulf adventures. The crossing would take four days, *inshallah*.

As usual Bob's celestial positions coincided with my instinctive ones. On the third day at sea we crossed the Mombasa-bound freighter *Dahlia*. Her captain, a friend of mine, confirmed our position. We landed in Aldabra on the afternoon of the following day and while my friends surfed ashore over the reef I sailed the *Mir-El-Lah* inside the lagoon. I shouted to them, '*Veille l'embellie*,' as they crossed the breakers – but they could not hear me. I told Kimuyu that fishing was prohibited. The fish here were protected. He could not understand this, so I removed the hook from the feather jig and let him tease the fish. He soon discovered that it was more fun to play and feed them than to kill them. I told him the story of St Francis, and he told me he would like to meet him when he came to Kilifi.

The scientists on Aldabra went out of their way to make our stay pleasant; we lived with them in their corrugated-iron bungalows and enjoyed their showers and cold drinks. Bob and I dived in several places, hoping to find the wrecks mentioned by Captain Alphonse: we found many rare shells but no wrecks.

The *Mir-El-Lah* rode at anchor in the channel where in 1916 the German battleship *Koenigsberg* hid from the Royal Navy for many months. The tides there were strong like a river in spate and I feared they would break our moorings. The lagoon was filled with coral heads and narrow crevices running in all directions like underwater corridors. In places they formed large pools where we spent hours watching the life they contained. Nowhere before had I been able to feed and stroke game fish under water; they just glided around us, confident and unafraid. In the main channel we often swam with schools of 'mermaids', similar to large parrot fish, with wide pectorals and flipping tails, which dived and surfaced like humans. Swimming with them was like being amongst silent aquatic people from another planet.

No day was like the next; the sea and the landscape changed colour and shape with each tide as the water slipped over the coral flats. In the magic moment of dusk I often sailed far away in the 'pram' so that I could gaze at the *Mir-El-Lah* lost in this luminous space. At night, at the turn of the tide when the sea stood still, we could hear the sounds of the lagoon: birds calling, fish splashing in the water, and the waves crashing beyond the reef.

The ring of the atoll was made up of a mini-world of green valleys thick with undergrowth, palms and casuarina trees. Giant crabs lived in cracks in the coral. At dusk over the reefs the frigate birds waylaid home-coming boobies in acrobatic aerial battles, forcing them to spit out the fish they had brought home for their young. A large colony of frigates nested on several *champignons* near the dhow (a *champignon*, 'mushroom', is a pillar of coral corroded at the base by the sea; surrounded as they are by water, they make ideal nesting-places).

Two weeks later we sailed for Astove; half-way there we met heavy black clouds advancing low on the water. The sun flashed pillars of light through them, the sea began to rise fast. I remembered that Astove had no shelter or anchorage; it was a place one could approach only in the best of weather conditions. I altered my course for Assumption Island, ten miles to the south. As night fell we sailed into a bay well protected from the storm

Overleaf Like many others I dreamed of restoring this house and living there for ever

approaching from the east. After a few hours and a wild burst of heavy rain, the clouds raced on towards the west and we basked in one of the many astonishing sunsets so characteristic of this part of the world.

Assumption is a rocky island fifty feet high ringed by a white beach. Opposite the dhow was a house just like the house that I had drawn with coloured pencils when I was a child, with one door, two windows, a chimney, and a path leading from the door into some bushes. A man with a wide-brimmed straw hat came down the path to meet us; he was the superintendent of the island, Monsieur Antoine, and behind him, at a respectable distance, stood a few Africans wearing tattered shorts.

Monsieur Antoine supervised fifty slaves, known euphemistically as 'black volunteers', who dug and collected phosphate powder in wells sunk deep into the coral ledge in the centre of the island. Their pay was low, and when they went home once a year they blew what money they had on drinks in a few days and returned as 'new recruits' on the same schooner to Assumption. On the beach, beside the superintendent's house, was a cemetery for those who died there. Beyond the white beach and the palm trees, men were being buried alive in dusty pits, wasting their lungs and consuming their bodies for a handful of money.

Mirella and I tried to persuade Monsieur Antoine to make a protest about these working conditions, but the thin, frail superintendent hardly listened. He was concerned more about a troublesome molar which he begged me to extract. He gave me a pair of pliers. I pulled hard, but was afraid of smashing his upper jaw. I twisted the instrument and heard a crunch: I had managed to pulverise the crown of his molar, leaving the root inside. As soon as he was able to speak again he told me he felt better. A black volunteer immediately came forward and pointed to his row of gleaming white teeth, but I had had enough of dentistry and retreated hastily to the *Mir-El-Lah.* We left Monsieur Antoine and his 'volunteers' with regrets; they were fine people, ruthlessly exploited.

Cosmoledo lay forty miles to the east and we were running short of time, for Bob and Tuesday had booked their return flights to Paris from Mombasa for February 3rd. Cruising in the southern Indian Ocean and keeping business appointments in Paris were hardly compatible.

Cosmoledo's wide open lagoon has two entrances; we chose La Passe du Nord as it is easier to navigate; but the tides were gentler than at Aldabra, so there was really no problem.

It is difficult to describe Cosmoledo without using clichés: dream-like, paradisal, incredible, unbelievable ... The lagoon is almost circular and seven miles long; we anchored in the middle of it. The ring of land around supports the usual palm trees, casuarinas and bright green shrubs where thousands of sea birds nest. There are long white powdery spits of sand which at high tide are covered with only a few inches of water; like a mirror, they send out sparkling refractions which differ with the angle of the sun. There are moments when a man walking there looks twice as large as life and seems to be floating in space. There seemed to be much wind high up, and we saw spectacular displays of racing clouds. Perhaps it was the monsoon hitting the colder regions of the southern hemisphere as it travelled northwards, pushing the rains to India. I never thought of cyclones; I was absorbed by the beauty of the sky. From morning till sunset the display of clouds never ceased to amaze me. One night at full moon I buried myself in the sand, leaving only my mouth and eyes out. I stared up into the sky for a long time. I saw an explosion among the stars; way, way up there was a tremendous flash as if two of them had collided.

The south side of the atoll was inhabited by six fishermen who arrived to greet us in a whaler, rowing with short rhythmical strokes. Kimuyu prepared Bajun tea for everybody while they told us, in archaic French *patois*, that they had been there for six months catching and drying fish, and that they had no women with them. We mentioned wrecks and one of them offered to take us to the schooner *Meredith White*, which Captain Alphonse of *La Belle Vue* had spoken of as having sunk off Cosmoledo in 1800.

The next day we found the wreck without difficulty. A large colony of green turban-shaped snails lived on her twisted remains. The size of a small melon, they are the prime source of mother-of-pearl. Despite a strong swell that made diving rather difficult we collected this treasure from the sea.

The southern part of the lagoon is very shallow, a large white expanse covered by only a few inches of water. Wading there is a unique experience; I collected many cowrie shells, beautifully discoloured by the sun through the shallow water. Their usually dark brown markings were now a pale pinkish-beige.

Thousands of boobies nested in the bushes on the outer ring of the atoll. It was the hatching season, and fluffy white chicks trembled in their nests while their mothers protested at our intrusion with shrill, high-pitched cries and occasional jabs with their powerful beaks. A flight of plovers rose in front of us, and skimmed low over the water, taking off and landing in rhythm with their leader.

One day as the tide was coming in Bob and I made a memorable dive at

Overleaf The Kartala explosion in Grande Comore marked the 'grand finale' of the Voyage of the *Mir-El-Lah*

the mouth of La Grande Passe. We followed the current, running at a speed of four to five knots, and glided underwater with silver barracudas darting about or floating in the flowing river. We spread our arms like wings and twisted, turned, dived and soared like birds.

Bob's Paris deadline was a thorn in our sides – it was a most unnatural situation, like swimming against the current – and back to Mombasa we had to go. That, at least, was the intention: but events turned out otherwise.

21. Shipwreck

The weather was menacing as we approached Aldabra to pick up John, one of the members of the Royal Society's station returning to Mombasa with us. I guessed – wrongly – that it was the monsoon. Monsoon means 'season'; it's not a wind. During these seasons the winds in our latitude seldom reach gale force unless a hurricane strikes. At Aldabra I was told that no cyclone warning had been received from Madagascar. We set sail at night in a rough, uncomfortable sea; heavy rain fell while we were still in sight of land. Mafia Island was four hundred miles to the north-east, and Dar-es-Salaam a few more miles to the north.

After a bad night I was still trying to climb up and down the waves rolling down from the north. In the early morning I saw a wave twice as big as any of the others coming our way; I reduced speed to dead slow and grabbed the wheel with all my strength as the watery mountain slammed into the dhow like a liquid punch. The *Mir-El-Lah* rose by her bows until we were almost vertical and I feared she would sink stern first or capsize backwards. After a few thrilling moments she settled in the trough. I turned to run before the wind: I could no longer hide from myself the fact that we were in bad trouble and I was fighting to save our lives. We could capsize so easily.

We were sailing south towards Madagascar, the Mozambique Channel and the Comoro Islands. We could set the lateen now and save fuel. I estimated our position some two hundred miles off the African coast, south of Mafia Island and four hundred miles north of the Comores. We aimed for the Grande Comore, the largest of four islands a few miles apart. Grande Comore consists mainly of a three-thousand-foot volcano, the Kartala; according to the *Pilot*, on a clear day it can be sighted from a hundred miles away: not an easy place to miss, even in a storm.

Colin Mudie's words suggesting I add ten tons of ballast returned to my mind; I was learning the hard way. On the afternoon of the third day Bob was able to get a fix at noon and worked out our position: according to his calculations we were two hundred and seventy miles from Grande Comore. Were we?

Sooner or later every sailor runs into a storm. I tried to keep calm and

Overleaf The *Mir-El-Lah* at low tide, shipwrecked on
Grande Comore. I swore I would refloat her

confident as a *nakhoda* should: I was past trying to give reasons or find excuses. My gallant crew of Africans were fatalistic and I could see they were prepared to accept death without too much of a struggle. I saw a huge wave catching up on us. I shouted a warning to John at the wheel. He shouted something back to me but I did not understand what he was saying. The steering-cable had snapped; the *Mir-El-Lah* broached rapidly. I ordered Bob, Kimuyu and Mirella to control the tiller by hand while I helped Madeka repair the wheel's cable.

A strange sea was building up from the south-east conflicting with the normal south-bound run of the north-eastern monsoon. Rain squalls and cold winds were hitting us once every hour while we were being pushed towards the south-east, the very place I wanted to avoid. I could afford to miss the Comoro Islands but not Madagascar. Beyond that lay a vast emptiness down to the South Pole. Despite my lack of sleep I felt in good shape; my adrenalin kept me going. It is amazing what men can do when they have no option.

Suddenly the engine stopped. Within seconds Madeka was in the engine-room shouting to me that the gear box had seized up; its oil had seeped out. I disengaged the gears; the engine was still thumping. Madeka filled the empty gear box with a can of oil he had found floating in the bilge. I slammed in the forward gear and we moved on again. Despite the strong wind we decided to hoist the mainsail to save fuel and be ready for further engine failures. With bleeding hands we pushed the boom and the sail skywards. Suddenly steering was easier and the *Mir-El-Lah* raced along majestically as on the day I sailed from Sirri island to Dubai with the *shamal*. But I did not dare switch off the engine; the battery was submerged and was certainly dead.

Half an hour later I heard a violent crack overhead. Forty feet above the deck the sixty-foot boom had snapped in half, and the two pieces hung down, folded like the wings of a stricken bird. A splinter of wood slashed into the rubber dinghy, opening a gash in its side. The sail flapped madly and we had to cut down the cracked boom, fouled at the top of the mast. The only person who could climb it was Juma, whom we'd hired at the last moment in Kilifi, but he refused. I tried to reason with him, explaining that our lives were at stake, including his. He was adamant. In the slashing rain Mirella, Madeka and Kimuyu argued with him in Swahili, but Juma just shrugged his shoulders. I took him aside and gave him a hundred Kenyan shillings (five pounds). Without a word he took off his shirt, prepared a coiled rope, held a knife in his teeth and climbed the mast like a child shinning up a coconut palm. Despite the strong wind and heavy roll he reached the top and slashed the boom free as we watched transfixed by his calm dexterity. He slid down, returned the knife to me and asked for a cigarette.

*

The *Mir-El-Lah* was breaking up at the stern. The upper deck made of thick *mavuli*, an African teak, weighed several tons and each roll unhinged the hull a little more. The squeaking finally turned into a splintering noise, and we had to join the two bulwarks at the stern with a chain tourniquet to keep the boat from splitting. I briefly considered cutting off the upper deck and pushing it overboard, but we had no axes.

By now we had been at sea for five days and four nights, and according to Bob's navigation and my reckoning we should have been well in sight of Grande Comore. Despite the clouds, we should see this huge black mountain any moment, and until we did I could not rest or relax; I was afraid, though, that if I did not sleep soon I might collapse.

Madeka announced that he had poured the last gallon of oil into the gear-box. Our old pump was emptying water at a fantastic rate. The speed latch had failed. The engine was racing at twice the allowed revolutions with the high-pitched whine of a chain saw. For how long? The time had come when a sailor must turn to God for help. I felt I had to offer Him something worthy of His intervention. What? Suddenly I knew. I would never touch a woman again for the rest of my life. I lifted my eyes skywards and said, 'Oh God, I was about to fool You. You know I cannot keep this promise. Our fate is written in the stars. Thy will be done and amen.'

My conversation with God was interrupted by John, who whispered in my wet ear that he thought he had sighted land. I handed the wheel over to Bob and ran forward. It was late afternoon and the sky was dark grey, with clouds changing shape and melting with the dimming light. After some long intense looking, I saw way up in the sky a solid contour that remained steadily unchanged. It was Kartala, Grandè Comore, and we were barely two miles away from its outer reef. I shouted 'L-A-A-A-N-D' as many desperate sailors have in the past (and in the movies).

Within minutes Kimuyu and Mirella had managed to brew a cup of coffee and we drank to the land we had sighted. We were facing the eastern side of Kartala, and the wind and rain were lashing us harder than ever. I tried to follow a course parallel to this unwelcoming shelterless island. When the light was gone, John and I kept watch on deck, motoring slowly down the coast following the reef. Half-way up this frightening mountain and looming into the clouds above us was one light: the Cyclops' eye.

At dawn I sighted the southernmost tip of the island and, keeping the reef two hundred yards to starboard, I followed its contour sailing west towards Moroni harbour. The *Pilot* said that at a place called Kapini there was a crack in the reef and with 'local knowledge' it was possible to sail through it for shelter. I believed this to be on the lee side of the island and was surprised when the *Mir-El-Lah* was again lashed by gusts of wind that whipped the sea into foamy crests like those we had experienced before. Beyond the reef the coast was a jagged mass of black sharp lava rocks. Nowhere could we land with a rubber dinghy, or even swim ashore.

I could see people on the beach near a village. Two men were launching a dugout canoe in a tract of sheltered water behind a spit of lava. Waving their paddles to us, they pointed towards the outer reef. At slow speed I sailed as close to it as possible. Obviously they were trying to show us the passage through the reef mentioned in the *Pilot*. They paddled between the shore and the reef and, when they were in the channel, stopped and raised the paddles in the air. Surfing on a wave, I held my breath while we sailed in and found ourselves in calmer water at last. I followed the canoe along this small passage until the men waved at me to drop anchor. We were now trapped between two reefs and, although we ourselves were saved, *Mir-El-Lah* was still in grave danger. It was now low tide, but at high tide the outer reef could not stop the waves from rushing in. The pump had packed up two hours before and, even if the two anchors held, the dhow was rapidly filling with water. To save the *Mir-El-Lah* it was now essential to beach her.

I began disembarking everybody, together with our most precious possessions. Like vultures, the villagers on the black volcanic shore formed a line of thin, scrawny people, with small children holding their hands. I was afraid that if the *Mir-El-Lah* broke up on the reef they would move in to scavenge anything they could find. They seemed famished, and it looked as if our death was to be their life. Their village was nothing more than a shanty town built with drift-wood and other flotsam.

A teenager wearing a T-shirt with *Jeunesse Revolutionaire* written on it told me he was chief of the village and he suggested we leave our belongings in the Maison du Peuple where it would be safe. Leaving Kimuyu to guard our bags I returned to the dinghy. Two hundred yards away the *Mir-El-Lah* rode at anchor. I would go to Moroni to look for help, and arrange for Air Comores to fly my friends with Mirella and Amina to Mombasa. I told Madeka that if the dhow broke her anchors at high water they must save their lives before anything else. I gave some money to the fishermen who had guided us inside the reef and asked them to stay and help my crew.

In the lorry on the road to Moroni I twitched nervously and could not sleep or relax. The road climbed up the slopes of the Kartala. Far down below the sea was foaming; even on land the wind raced around the hills, rising steadily in pitch. I could single out the squalls, scattered like mushrooms over the ocean, pouring rain over the waves.

At Moroni, a small Islamic town with a touch of French provincial atmosphere, we were taken to the house of 'La Jeunesse Revolutionaire' and after a short explanation were admitted to the new 'Etat Comorien' whose President, Ali Soilih, was nicknamed 'the Madman of Moroni'. I rushed to the 'harbour' for help. The harbour consisted of a cement jetty behind which a war-time landing-craft was being battered by the waves. They hit the top of a thirty-foot lighthouse built on a rock near the end of the jetty. A tarmac road winding between a long row of three-storeyed houses and the sea was being swept away in places; soon the houses themselves would be in danger. At sea I had imagined this useless harbour as the place of salvation, the abode of peace and rest. Nobody was around except for a few idle onlookers, children and old men.

Suddenly I collapsed; I had not slept or eaten much for five days. My body gave up, my legs folded and I began shaking and chattering as if I had malaria. I felt a desperate need for blankets to keep me warm. Mirella took me to the Itsandra Hotel.

I was still coherent, but I found myself hating the dhow, hating her with all my heart. I hoped she would sink and disappear from my life. I was feverish and fell asleep for a few hours. When I awoke I tried to be rational and told Bob to go to Kapini and beach the dhow at high tide. I told him exactly what to do: sail over the reef, get into the bay, turn around, face the waves, drop the anchors and reverse one hundred yards towards the beach. Position the boat there, tie two stern-lines to the palms and pray. I knew that by giving these instructions I was deserting the *Mir-El-Lah*. I could not find the spark that would move me from my bed because I really did not want to: I hoped the *Mir-El-Lah* would die.

Twelve hours later when Bob and Mirella came back I sensed immediately that the *Mir-El-Lah* was lost. He said that the sea had been very rough and the wind strong. They had followed my instructions but the dhow was now sideways and . . . I interrupted him to ask if they had dropped the big emergency anchor. When Bob said, no, they did not think about it, I closed my eyes. I knew that the hand of God had played a role in all this. The *Mir-El-Lah* was lost.

At six next morning Mirella woke me up. Madeka had arrived to say that the *Mir-El-Lah* had sunk. He came into my room dripping wet; he was crying. I had never seen him cry before.

I stood up, feeling better; my fever had gone. I told Mirella to remain in Moroni and fly to Mombasa on the next available plane with Amina, Bob and Tuesday. John and my crew would stay with me and I would go to Kapini to assess the situation. The loss of the *Mir-El-Lah* had been entirely my fault and my collapse had been a very convenient excuse to wash my hands of the whole affair.

When I arrived at Kapini I saw my dhow rolling on her side, half submerged and hit by powerful waves. All her contents were strewn across the pebbly beach or floating in the water, being washed on and off the shore. Something happened inside me, as if I had seen Mirella herself drowning and I decided that the *Mir-El-Lah* must be saved at all costs. I turned to John, the quiet, efficient Englishman, and asked him to remain on the spot and lighten the dhow by removing everything on board. I would go back to Moroni, hire a few carpenters and bring them back with tools and timber. We would patch up the *Mir-El-Lah* at low tide and she would float again. From that moment on there were no longer days and nights in my life, only low and high tides.

The storm was still raging, and at Moroni airport I found out that the weather forecast was bad for days to come. Two cyclones, Fifi and Emily, were sweeping over Madagascar less than a hundred miles away to the south. Reality had caught up with me.

Kimuyu and Madeka built two huts on the beach with the flotsam we had saved or that was being washed ashore. In fact the villagers helped, not being at all the hostile scavengers I had imagined them when we arrived. Mattresses, blankets, pillows and clothes were spread over bushes to dry. Kimuyu had saved his stove, the gas bottles and most of his utensils. We would live on the beach until the *Mir-El-Lah* was afloat again, though the chances that this would happen seemed slim.

The trip to Moroni and back was twenty-five miles by twisting roads and dilapidated transport. I returned with three carpenters and began to dismantle and hack to pieces the upper deck, the prime cause of the collapse of the transom. With the help of many of the villagers we completed the job at low tide. The carpenters, real dhow-builders, assessed the situation and immediately knew what to do; they were convinced that, *inshallah*, we would save the *Emir Allah*.

We worked at night by the light of several hurricane-lamps and a few

Shipwrecked on Grande Comore with Bob

torches I had salvaged from the wreck. When the seas hammered and often destroyed what we had just repaired we rested in the huts which Kimuyu and Madeka had made comfortable and cosy. They had even erected a kitchen, with a roof made from one of the sails.

With the help of Philippe Perrin, his wife and some other new local friends we tried and failed to right the boat, which was stuck with the bow facing the beach, offering the stern to the onrushing waves. I tied eight forty-four-gallon drums under the keel to add buoyancy to the hull; John and I pulled on the anchor chains, steel cables, nylon cords, and a turfer, improvising giant tourniquets; the carpenters patched and caulked the planking until the water was up to their necks. If any of those overworked, overstretched cables had snapped, any of us could have been sliced in half.

The *Mir-El-Lah* remained fast on the rocks, which held her like a vice. We dug under her keel and inserted four tree trunks beneath her belly. Not even the raging waves smashing against her hulk could move her. I began then to lose hope.

Then the weather improved. The storm had passed. I got hold of the tide tables and found out that towards the end of February we would have one of the highest tides of the year at four in the morning – in the dark. The night of the high tide was a starry one, warm, gentle as the sea lapping at our ankles and caressing the dhow. Ten minutes before the highest tide we pulled and pushed with all our strength, straining all cables to breaking-point. No way: fifty tons of *Mir-El-Lah* were stuck firm on the lava rocks. We still had a few more minutes of hope; I could not unclench my fists. Suddenly the keel began sliding down the beach; we all cheered. Our overstretched cables were pulling, sucking the dhow into deeper water. She was floating! Stripped to her barest essentials, scarred, dismasted, but floating and alive!

We turned the bows towards the ocean and got her over the smaller outer reef. At dawn Jeannot, a diesel mechanic, stripped the engine down to clean and dry it as best he could. It had been submerged in salt water for nearly a month. When he fired it with two new batteries he had brought from Moroni, the engine spat out a huge cloud of black smoke, coughed for a while and spluttered back to life.

Looming above the menacing black shape of Kartala looked down on us from a pale blue sky, and across the bay we could see the island of Moheli twenty miles away. We sailed to Moroni, and the day after our arrival there the Kartala erupted. A new crater half-way up its western side began to spew out a torrent of flaming lava down her slopes, cutting off the road to Kapini. The tropical forest I had crossed so many times was reduced to a barren plateau of black molten lava. At night while the earth shook and rumbled the sky was the backdrop for a display of giant fireworks.

Jeannot and I drove up the mountain road, left the car and walked to the new crater. The light was white and vivid as on a movie set. Suddenly the earth shook again and the fire in the sky doubled in size; I thought we were about to be swallowed by the flames. From nearby villages people ran screaming downhill, and Jeannot and I regained the car. I had to steady his hand so that he could open the door and insert the ignition key. As we drove down I kept looking back to check the direction of the lava flow. We returned to the harbour to spend the night on the dhow: if the lava came our way the *Mir-El-Lah* would save our lives at sea. We spent the night gazing at the fires, smelling the sulphurous air. *Allah akbah, Allah karim* ... These words were on my lips all the time.

I could not attempt to cross from the Comores to Mombasa with the *Mir-El-Lah* in her present condition. The solution to my dilemma came from a stranger who approached me on the pier at Moroni, a Frenchman who was manager of a Coca Cola bottling plant on the island of Anjouan. He asked me point blank if I would consider ferrying two thousand cases of empty bottles to Anjouan and bring them back full.

I did not know the Coca Cola capacity of my dhow. The standard way to measure a dhow's cargo space was based on date 'packages'. I reckoned if the *Mir-El-Lah* could hold two thousand packages of dates from the Shatt-al-Arab she should hold two thousand cases of Coca Cola bottles from Anjouan. I told the man to wait and raced to my friend Jean Claude Favetto's house, where I found him conversing with Jeannot.

Would they be interested in running Coca Cola from Anjouan to Moroni? I told them about the offer and suggested that Jeannot would make a good *nakhoda* with the help of a local crew. After all, there are only sixty miles from Anjouan to Grande Comore, with Mohéli half-way in between.

Two hours and many handshakes later, Jean Claude, Jeannot, Hassan Soilihi – a local Arab merchant with a good knowledge of dhows – and myself were in business. Within two days the first two thousand Coca Cola cases were on board; we also loaded two cars, fifty sacks of sugar and two cows. The *Mir-El-Lah* had reverted to what she had been built for: a work-horse of the sea.

I was now able to return to Kenya, rest awhile and learn how to live without the *Mir-El-Lah*. Although my dhow was refloated and actually working for me, I had agreed to share her ownership with my three friends from Moroni. She was no longer mine. I saw her sailing away to Anjouan with Jeannot at the helm and her new crew waving and cheering. Silently, discreetly, staring ahead lest my friends detect the tears streaming down my face, I wept. Like saying goodbye to a lover, I felt cruel, proud, happy, unhappy, delivered, free, lonely and confused.

The *Mir-El-Lah* worked for us for several months and I received my share of money regularly – a tidy sum – which she was earning in the Coca Cola trade. And then one day a telegram arrived from Moroni stating laconically that the *Mir-El-Lah* had been hijacked by political prisoners who had escaped from the clutches of Ali Soilih, the Madman of Moroni, (who shortly afterwards was assassinated). The telegram concluded with the news that the hijackers had set sail towards the island of Madagascar.

Can anyone tell me what's happened to the *Mir-El-Lah*? I'd like to know.

Glossary

ABUBUZ: dhow with a long bowsprit, inspired by a trading schooner

AGHAL: rope to hold headcloth

ALLAH AKBAR: God is great

ALLAH KARIM: God is merciful

BAGHLA or BAGGALA: large dhow with five ports (windows) in the square stern, built mostly in Sur (Oman)

BAJUN: native of the islands of Lamu

BANDAR: harbour

BELAT: land wind from Hadhramaut

BHANG: Cannabis indica

BOOM: deep-sea dhow

BORITI: mangrove poles

BUIBUI: woman's black garment

BWANA: Sir, Mister

CHAI: tea

DISH-DASH: loose Arab garment

EMIR: ruling chieftain

HAJJI: one who has made the pilgrimage to Mecca

HALWA: sweetmeat

INGALAO: outrigger canoe with small lateen sail

INSHALLAH: if God pleases

JABAL: mountain

JAHAZI: coastal Lamu dhow

JALBOOT: small dhow from Bahrein and Kuwait, often used on the pearl banks

JAMBO (Swahili): hullo

KAZI-KAZI (Swahili): strong wind

KEBIR: big

KHALIL: small

KHANJAR: curved dagger

KIKOI: colourful length of cotton worn round the waist, or as a dress by men and women on the East African coast

LATEEN: triangular sail

MLANGO (Swahili): literally 'door', passage through the reef

MUALLIMU: learned man, priest (also ship's mate)

NAKHODA: dhow captain
NGOMA (Swahili): dance
RAS: cape (geographical)
RUUS: literally 'head', peak of a mountain
SALAAM ALEIKUM: greetings to you (response 'aleikum salaam')
SAMBUK: square-sterned dhow
SEKONI: helmsman of a dhow
SERANG: boatswain
SHAMAL: north wind
SHARGI: south wind
SHIFTA: raiders from Somaliland and Ethiopia
SUCRAM: thank you
SWAHILI: natives of the East Coast of Africa and their language
TAIJIB: good

Index